CONTENTS

Introduction

Coping with Depression is the sixty-eighth volume in the **Issues** series. The aim of this series is to offer up-to-date information about important issues in our world.

Coping with Depression examines the different types of depression, its causes and treatment.

The information comes from a wide variety of sources and includes:
Government reports and statistics
Newspaper reports and features
Magazine articles and surveys
Web site material
Literature from lobby groups
and charitable organisations.

It is hoped that, as you read about the many aspects of the issues explored in this book, you will critically evaluate the information presented. It is important that you decide whether you are being presented with facts or opinions. Does the writer give a biased or an unbiased report? If an opinion is being expressed, do you agree with the writer?

Coping with Depression offers a useful starting-point for those who need convenient access to information about the many issues involved. However, it is only a starting-point. At the back of the book is a list of organisations which you may want to contact for further information.

*****

Coping with Depression

ISSUES

Volume 68

Editor

Craig Donnellan

 **Independence**

Educational Publishers
Cambridge

First published by Independence
PO Box 295
Cambridge CB1 3XP
England

© Craig Donnellan 2003

British Library Cataloguing in Publication Data
Coping with Depression – (Issues Series)
I. Donnellan, Craig II. Series
616.8'527

ISBN 1 86168 250 6

Printed in Great Britain
MWL Print Group Ltd

Typeset by
Claire Boyd

Cover
The illustration on the front cover is by
Pumpkin House.

Depression

Information from SANE

Depression has been called the 'common cold of psychiatry' because it is by far the most frequently encountered mental illness. Most people suffer low spirits when things keep going wrong but, though they may be temporarily depressed, they recover quickly. This brief taste of depression is very different from *depressive illness*, which is long-lasting and severe and needs professional help to recover. Many doctors now believe that depressive illness is a physical condition caused by some fault in brain chemistry which makes sufferers predisposed to severe depression. The illness may then be triggered by stress, physical illness, drug abuse and the like. There are no laboratory tests for depression so doctors can diagnose only from your behaviour. And since depressive illness, and simple reversible depression from which we all suffer at times, cover wide ranges of severity, it may be hard to distinguish the least severe cases of depressive illness from a bad attack of the 'blues'.

How common is depression?

Depressive illness is very common although there are no reliable figures. The picture is like that of an iceberg. The small part above the water represents cases that have been diagnosed and are not in doubt. The great bulk beneath the water represents depressed people who have not sought help.

The US National Institute of Mental Health estimated that in any year, 15% of (US) adults aged 18 to 74 suffer serious depressive illness. In Britain, the Royal College of Psychiatrists say that 1 in 20 adults (5%) suffers from depressive illness *at any one time*, which is broadly similar to the US experience when you take into account that most attacks last a few months. The Royal College also surveyed a sample of 2000 adults (15 years upwards) and found that 22% claimed they had suffered from depression *at some time in their lives*.

Doctors treat about 3% of their practice list for depression in a year and refer one in ten to psychiatrists. Depressive illness is almost twice as common in women as in men. In Britain, 3-4% of men and 7-8% of women suffer from moderate to severe depressive illness at any one time.

Depressive disorders occur in all social classes and at all ages from childhood to old age. The severe forms are more common in middle and old age but those in their 20s and 30s are now known to have more depressive illness than had previously been thought. It is uncommon in

---

Most people suffer low spirits when things keep going wrong but, though they may be temporarily depressed

---

children although cases do occasionally occur, especially among teenage girls.

Some people believe the growing amount of stress in our lives is causing a corresponding increase in depressive illness but there are no reliable figures to support this.

Symptoms of depression

The symptoms of a depressive disorder are a mixture of mood changes and despair with anxiety and physical problems. Before a diagnosis can be made, the symptoms should persist and be overwhelming over at least two weeks.

The major feature of all depression is a marked change of mood, a feeling of hopelessness about the future and a preoccupation with gloomy thoughts of death and disaster. The sufferer loses interest in life, may talk of suicide, is unable to concentrate and frequently tearful.

These depressive symptoms are often accompanied by those of anxiety, which may include loss of appetite and weight (which can be severe), constipation, decline in

sexual interest, headaches, sleep-lessness, loss of energy and tiredness. Anxiety symptoms are sometimes the most prominent, even though their cause is a depressive illness. As many as 40% of people suffering from depression visit their doctor in the first place for treatment of these secondary symptoms.

Symptoms of depressive illness

Mood changes
- Low mood, sadness
- Tearfulness
- Hopelessness about the future
- Preoccupation with gloomy thought, death and disaster
- Feeling that life is not worth living; thoughts of suicide
- Irrational guilt about past actions
- Inability to concentrate for long
- Loss of social interest and motivation

Anxiety
- Physical symptoms: palpitations, churning stomach etc.
- Fear of non-dangerous situations
- Panic attacks
- Persistent worrying out of proportion to causes

What makes depression more likely?

Social factors
- Being unemployed
- Coming from an economically poor background
- Having a recent setback (bereavement, divorce etc.)
- Being unable to confide in spouse or partner
- Having several young children at home
- Suffering from a chronic disabling or painful illness
- Being socially isolated, particularly in later life

Psychological factors
- Having experienced rejection in childhood
- Setting unattainable high standard for self or others
- Suffering chronic anxiety

Physical factors
- Having glandular fever, influenza or other illnesses
- Drinking excessive amounts of alcohol
- Having recently given birth
- Having a genetic disposition to depression
- Being poorly nourished
- Following life-threatening or mutilating surgery

Some hints on self-help in depressive illness
- Try to understand the illness and be positive about it
- Be honest with your counsellor or doctor. Tell him or her the truth about what you think may have caused it
- Find some things you enjoy and which temporarily make you feel less depressed
- Try to maintain your appearance, your home and your personal relationships
- Avoid alcohol and non-prescribed drugs
- Eat a reasonable diet even if you are not always hungry
- Involve a relative, friend or spouse in your therapy
- Talk to friends, relatives, your doctor or counsellor about your problems and do your best to avoid stress

■ The above information is an extract from SANE's web site which can be found at www.sane.org.uk

© SANE 2003

Stressed Britain

45% of those who have felt stressed in Britain have been depressed as a consequence

New stress research by MORI to mark the start of Samaritans Week shows, among other things, Britain is smoking, drinking and slobbing out to cope with high daily stress levels.

Samaritans, the emotional support charity, today announced the results of new research into stress in the UK and Republic of Ireland carried out by MORI to mark the start of its awareness and fundraising week, held between 17 and 24 May 2003.

The research shows that one in five people in Great Britain experiences stress on a daily basis and that the emotional consequences are severe, with a quarter of people who are stressed feeling isolated by

SAMARITANS

it, nearly half feeling depressed or down, and one in eight believing they have nowhere to turn.

The *Stressed Out* survey, which was carried out in England, Scotland and Wales to mark Samaritans Week found that the biggest causes of stress were jobs, money, family and health. However, it also showed that for one in eight of those who get stressed, violence in society is one of the biggest causes of stress, for one in seven the future on behalf of the next generation is worrying and for

one in 10, it is the use of drugs in today's society that causes stress. Other causes of stress ranged from the NHS to using public transport, to the slowness of the Internet or IT in general.

In addition, the survey showed that people in Britain deal with their stress in ways that may add to emotional distress in the long run. One of the ways most often chosen by a third of stressed Britons is to watch TV or listen to music, evading their problems, whilst nearly a quarter (23%) of Britons has an alcoholic drink, and just less than one in five (18%) have a cigarette. 15% of people simply adopt a British stiff upper lip, ignore their stress and get on with it.

Dr Raj Persaud, Consultant Psychiatrist at the Maudsley Hospital and Samaritans advocate, said, 'Whilst the levels of Britons who have been depressed or suicidal as a consequence of stress may seem shocking, in many ways, it's not surprising that modern life takes such a heavy toll on people today. People are subjected to a wide range of stressors and the social support structures that used to help people to cope by getting things off their chest, such as extended family and neighbours, no longer exist in the same way that they did. As the survey results show, this means that people are more likely to 'switch off' rather than trying to deal with the causes of their stress. There are better coping skills for dealing with stress than the ones most seem to be employing. And that's why Samaritans are more relevant than ever before in today's society.'

One of the ways most often chosen by a third of stressed Britons is to watch TV or listen to music, evading their problems

---

Chief Executive of Samaritans, Simon Armson, said, 'We would urge people to try to deal with stress as positively as they can rather than ignoring it, or turning to alcohol or smoking. If feelings are bottled up or ignored, they can lead to more severe emotional distress in the long run. Ultimately, by talking about problems it's possible to gain a sense of perspective that can make it easier to cope. During Samaritans Week, and every week, we are here 24 hours a day for everyone, everywhere.'

Notes

1. A nationally representative quota sample of 1,885 British adults aged 15+ were interviewed throughout Great Britain on the MORI Omnibus, across 191 sampling points. Interviews were carried out

using CAPI (Computer Assisted Personal Interviewing), face-to-face in respondents' homes between 3rd and 8th April 2003. Data have been weighted to reflect the known national population profile. Eighty-two per cent of British adults say they have ever felt stressed.

■ Samaritans is a registered charity, founded in 1953, which offers 24-hour confidential emotional support to anyone in emotional distress. Samaritans' vision is for a society where fewer people die by suicide because people are able to share feelings of emotional distress openly without fear of being judged. Samaritans believes that offering people the opportunity to be listened to in confidence, and accepted without prejudice, can alleviate

despair and suicidal feelings. It is the aim of Samaritans to make emotional health a mainstream issue. The service is offered by 18,300 trained volunteers and is entirely dependent on voluntary support.

Across the UK, you can call Samaritans on 08457 90 90 90 (1850 60 90 90 in the Republic of Ireland) for the price of a local call. You can also write to Samaritans at Chris, PO Box 9090, Stirling, FK8 2SA, send an e-mail to jo@samaritans.org or if you are deaf or hard of hearing use the single national minicom number 08457 90 91 92 (1850 60 90 91 in the Republic of Ireland).

'There are better coping skills for dealing with stress than the ones most seem to be employing. And that's why Samaritans are more relevant than ever before in today's society'

■ The above information is from the Samaritans' web site which can be found at www.samaritans.org.uk

© *The Samaritans*

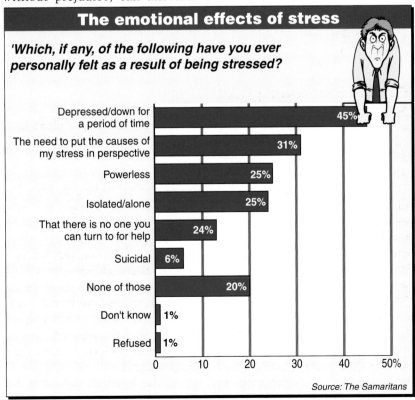

The emotional effects of stress

'Which, if any, of the following have you ever personally felt as a result of being stressed?'

Depressed/down for a period of time	45%
The need to put the causes of my stress in perspective	31%
Powerless	25%
Isolated/alone	25%
That there is no one you can turn to for help	24%
Suicidal	6%
None of those	20%
Don't know	1%
Refused	1%

Source: The Samaritans

Depression in children and young people

What is depression?

Depression is a common problem. It affects at least 2 in 100 children under 12 and 5 in every 100 teenagers. Depression is even more common in adults. Young people are much more likely to become depressed if they come from broken homes, have lost a parent in early life, have suffered from abuse or neglect or live in inner city areas where there are high rates of poverty, unemployment and crime. Depression is a serious and common illness but nowadays there is a great deal that can be done to help those affected by it. The first step to getting help is to be able to recognise the problem.

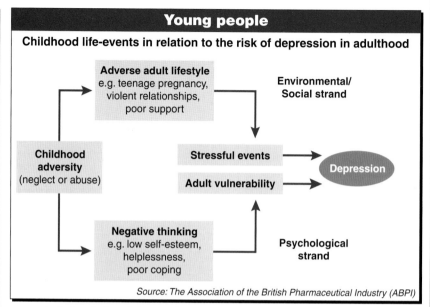

Young people

Childhood life-events in relation to the risk of depression in adulthood

Source: The Association of the British Pharmaceutical Industry (ABPI)

What effects can depression have?

Because depression affects so many aspects of life, your outlook, how you feel, what you are able to do, it can mean you cope with ordinary daily life much less well than usual. Depression can cause serious problems, such as:

- Difficulties getting on with friends and family
- Loss of friends
- Loss of confidence and difficulty making decisions
- Inability to study, work and perform well in exams
- Difficulty with day-to-day tasks
- Eating problems, turning to food for comfort and eating too much or dieting excessively
- Lying, stealing and truanting

Depression can sometimes be dangerous, increasing the risk of:

- Drug, alcohol or solvent abuse
- Self-injury such as drug overdose and wrist cutting
- Suicide

What causes depression?

Depression is commonly caused by a mixture of things, rather than any one thing alone.

- Some people have experiences that lead to depression. These include family breakdown, abuse, neglect and bullying. Serious illness and the death or loss of a loved one can also cause depression.
- People are more 'at risk' of becoming depressed if they have no one to share their worries with a lot of demands on them, and not enough support.
- Depression often 'runs in families' and someone with a close relative who is affected by depression has a higher risk of becoming depressed themselves. Girls and women are more likely than boys and men to become depressed.

Warning signs

It is important to distinguish ordinary tiredness, stress and sadness from the onset of clinical depression. If you are worried that you, or someone you know, might be getting depressed, these are some of the warning signs to look out for:

- Tiredness and loss of energy
- Persistent sadness
- Loss of self-confidence and self-esteem
- Difficulty concentrating
- Not being able to enjoy things that are usually pleasurable or interesting
- Undue feelings of guilt or worthlessness
- Sleeping problems – difficulties in getting off to sleep or waking up much earlier than usual
- Avoiding other people, sometimes even your close friends
- Finding it hard to concentrate at work/college/school
- Loss of appetite
- Loss of sex drive and/or sexual problems
- Physical aches and pains
- Thinking about suicide and death
- Self-harm

As a general rule, if you have experienced four or more of these symptoms, for most of the day nearly every day, for over two weeks or more, you should visit your GP as the first step in getting appropriate help.

What can help?

There are a lot of things that can be done to help people who suffer from depression. If you think that you or someone you know may be depressed, it's well worth asking for help. This means letting a caring adult know about the problem, and, if necessary, getting professional help. Family members can often provide valuable help and support. Teachers, school counsellors and school nurses can also be very helpful. Your family doctor may be able to help. He or she will also know about local services, and will be able to help you get the help that is needed.

Depression is a serious and common illness but nowadays there is a great deal that can be done to help those affected by it

---

Young people who are depressed often find it helpful to talk about their worries to a trained counsellor. Alternatively, depending on the problems and their causes, it may be helpful to seek advice and help from a member of the local child and family mental health team. Usually, these teams consist of specialists such as psychotherapists, psychiatrists, psychologists and social workers, all of whom are highly skilled in helping young people and their families. Getting effective help probably means sharing worries with someone who can help and putting heads together to work out new solutions and discover new ways of coping. Practical help may also be needed with, for example, relationships, school, finance and housing.

■ Depression Alliance is the leading UK charity for people with depression. We work to relieve and to prevent this treatable condition by providing information, support and understanding to those who are affected by it. We also campaign to raise awareness amongst the general public about the realities of depression. A member-led organisation, we have offices in England, Scotland and Wales.

For more information about Depression Alliance, our services, publications or membership scheme please contact your nearest office. Depression Alliance, 35 Westminster Bridge Road, London, SE1 7JB, Tel: 020 7633 0557. Fax: 020 7633 0559. E-mail: information@ depressionalliance.org. Web site: www.depressionalliance.org

Depression Alliance Scotland, 3 Grosvenor Gardens, Edinburgh, EH12 5JU. Tel: 0131 467 3050. Fax: 0131 467 7701.

Depression Alliance Cymru, 11 Plas Melin, Westbourne Road, Whitchurch, Cardiff, CF14 2BT. Tel: 029 2069 2891. Fax: 029 2052 1774.

Other useful organisations

The Samaritans: 0845 790 9090
Saneline: 0845 767 8000
CALL: 0800 132 737
SADA (SAD Association): 01903 814942
ChildLine: 0800 11 11
YoungMinds: 0800 018 2138

© *Depression Alliance*

Depression on the rise among young

Rate doubles for Generation X, study shows

The number of young people battling depression has doubled in 12 years, as hundreds of thousands find themselves excluded from rising levels of education and prosperity, according to a report today from the Joseph Rowntree Foundation.

Its researchers looked into how life has changed for men and women in their 20s, comparing a sample of 10,000 people in the so-called Generation X, born in 1970, with a previous survey of a similar number of baby boomers born in 1958.

Work for young people altered dramatically in the 12 years separating the two groups. Well over half the young people born in 1958 quit school at the minimum leaving age, and mostly moved into jobs and apprenticeships.

By 1986 the youth labour market in many parts of the country had collapsed. More 16-year-olds stayed in education, but those who did not were faced with youth training schemes, casual jobs, and unemployment.

The number gaining degree qualifications increased from 14% of men and 9% of women to 22% of men and 19% of women. Average earnings for young people born in 1970 were higher in real terms by the age of 25 than they had been for the group born in 1958. But earnings were not shared evenly. Experience of poverty as a child had an even greater adverse influence on the earnings of young adults born in 1970 than it had in the earlier generation.

The researchers from the institute of education at London University and the institute of employment research at Warwick University found the proportion of young people showing clear signs of depression doubled over the 12 years.

When those born in 1958 completed a questionnaire on their mental health in 1981, 7% had a tendency to non-clinical depression. The equivalent figure for the 1970 cohort, interviewed in 1996, was 14%. Analysis suggested that the rise was linked to the younger group having grown up with more experience of unemployment. Those with degrees were a third less likely to be depressed.

John Bynner, a director at the institute of education and an author of the report, said: 'The route to full-time employment has become more precarious in the past 25 years . . . Many more of the young people born in 1970 stayed on in education and gained qualifications. But those who left at the minimum age faced a future that was more uncertain and left them more prone to depression.'

Peter Elias of Warwick University, another of the authors, said socially disadvantaged young people aged between 15 and 25 needed more help than was on offer: 'We need to look afresh at the raft of initiatives since 1997, and refocus attention on the significant number of young people for whom expansion of higher education is not a solution.'

© *Guardian Newspapers Limited 2003*

Childhood depression

Ten per cent of all children will suffer a depressive episode before age 12. Few get help when they need it

Until the 1980s, it was generally thought that children could not become depressed. Now researchers recognise that children, like everyone else, are not immune from this insidious and dangerous disease. Because children often do not have the capacity to step back, look at themselves, and recognise that the way they're feeling isn't normal for them, diagnosis and treatment of depression is more difficult than for adults. It used to be thought that depression was caused by the loss of a loved one and the action of a punitive superego on the self – a harsh way of evaluating oneself against standards that are impossible to meet. But now it seems to be accepted that depression is much more complex than that, perhaps with a genetic component, certainly a psychophysiological disease that affects thought, emotions, behaviour, and the body.

Depression can present a confusing picture in children and adolescents. Sometimes children will let it be known that they feel hopeless, empty, or permanently sad – the signs we look for in adults. But more often children cannot express their feelings so directly and we must interpret their behaviour. Children, especially boys, may simply appear unusually angry or sullen. If this mood is unrelieved for more than a week, and especially if it does not seem to come in response to some real disappointment or loss, most likely the parent should seek help.

Other signs of depression in children include changes in appetite or energy level; sleeping a great deal more or less than usual; a drop in school performance; and excessive worrying. Especially worrisome is a loss of interest in things that used to give pleasure, as when a child seems not to care any longer for favourite toys or activities. Injuries that may seem accidental may have been the result of carelessness. The child may talk about death or thoughts of punishment.

One estimate which fits our experience is that 10 per cent of all children will suffer a depressive episode before age 12

Though it's clear now that preadolescent children do suffer from depression, the actual incidence is not known. Diagnosis is difficult. Estimates range from a few tenths of a per cent to the 15 to 20 per cent that is found in adults. One estimate which fits our experience is that 10 per cent of all children will suffer a depressive episode before age 12.

It's well recognised now that suicide, usually a result of depression whether diagnosed or not, is on the increase among teens. But thoughts or wishes of death, and self-destructive behaviour (often misinterpreted by adults as risky or dangerous play) are increasingly reported by young children. The idea that a child might think of taking his or her own life is horrifying and repugnant. And while we may be able to entertain the idea in theory, in real life when we run across such a child, perhaps in our own family, our denial kicks in.

Every child therapist can tell stories about seemingly caring parents who were unable or unwilling to take the simplest concrete steps – locking up medicines, getting rid of guns – to protect a suicidal child or adolescent. Therapists, teachers, physicians and others who know the child can get fooled as well, so that though a child or teen may sound seriously depressed to a neutral third party, we're so close to the picture that we don't get the complete message. I have talked with a surprising number of adults who remember suicide attempts as a child or teen. They were upset and hurt, felt that no one cared and that life wasn't worth living. They took a bottle of pills and went to sleep, expecting never to wake up. Fortunately, they weren't knowledgeable about the lethal dosage. Because they were convinced that no one cared, they told no one. But things got a little better, and they didn't repeat.

That's the best news about depression. It usually doesn't last too long. Patients usually respond well to treatment, both medication and psychotherapy. Parents can often make some adjustments in the way the family interacts to help a child or teen feel better.

The bad news is that so few get help when they need it. Among depressed adults, only one in three is treated. In one study of 27 severely disturbed teen suicide victims, only two were being treated when they died, and only one-third had ever been seen by a mental health professional.

■ The above information is from Undoing Depression's web site which can be found at www.undoingdepression.com

Young cannabis users at more risk of mental illness

By David Derbyshire, Science Correspondent

Teenagers who smoke cannabis are risking depression and schizophrenia later in life, three new studies conclude today.

Researchers have found that adolescents who use the drug at least once a week are increasing the chances of suffering serious mental illness. Girls are particularly at risk. One study found that smoking the drug each day increases the risks of depression five times; weekly use doubles the risk.

The links between cannabis and mental health have been debated for decades. But the new research, published today in the *British Medical Journal*, highlights the dangers to adolescents.

A study of 1,600 students in Australia between 1992 and 1998 found that frequent use of the drug led to depression and anxiety, particularly in girls. Around 60 per cent had used cannabis by the age of 20, and seven per cent said that they were daily users.

After taking into account other lifestyle factors, the researchers found that daily use increased the risk of depression fivefold in girls in young adulthood, while weekly use doubled the risk.

The research was led by Prof George Patton of the Murdoch Children's Research Institute, Parkville, Victoria. Prof Patton said: 'Strategies to reduce frequent use of cannabis might reduce the level of mental disorders in young people.'

> **One in ten of the people who used cannabis by the age of 15 in the sample developed schizophrenia by the time they were 26**

The other two studies looked at the links between cannabis and schizophrenia. One, led by Dr Stanley Zammit, of the University of Wales, Cardiff, found that cannabis increased the risk of schizophrenia by 30 per cent.

The study was of 50,000 Swedish conscripts carried out over 27 years. Self-medication with cannabis was an 'unlikely explanation' for the link, they found.

The third study found that the earlier teenagers start using cannabis, the greater the risk of schizophrenia. Those aged 15 in the study, led by researchers at King's College London, were four times more likely to have schizophrenia aged 26 than teenagers who did not use the drug.

One in ten of the people who used cannabis by the age of 15 in the sample developed schizophrenia by the time they were 26, compared with three per cent of later users and non-users, they found.

Marjorie Wallace, chief executive of the mental health charity Sane, said: 'While cannabis may be harmless to many people, there is no way of telling who might be the vulnerable victim for whom its use can turn from a relaxing trip into a lifelong torment.'

Ecstasy use triggers deep depression

Just two tablets enough to cause long-term health problems, psychologists are told

Ecstasy, the so-called love drug taken by hundreds of thousands each weekend, can result in crippling depression after just a couple of tablets, a study revealed yesterday.

Experts warned that the changes to the brain brought about by the drug leave a legacy of long-term mental health problems, including memory loss and lack of concentration, although many young people still regard it as harmless.

Psychologists have found that even those who gave up taking the drug several years ago scored higher on a depression rating than people who had never taken it.

But for clubbers who are taking large number of tablets regularly, ecstasy actually appears to tip them into clinical depression, according to Dr Lynn Taurah, researcher at London Metropolitan University.

She looked at the habits of 221 young professionals and studied the differences between frequent and less frequent ecstasy users, also comparing them with former users, people who used cannabis and those who took nothing at all.

'What we found is that, whether you have taken it fewer than 20 times or more than 20 times in the past few years, you are still more likely to be depressed than non-users,' said Taurah.

'But for those who over years have taken thousands of tablets, there is a significant chance of serious depression. It's a weird drug.'

By Jo Revill, Health Editor

'At first it gives you a surge of happiness, but after a day or two, and up to three weeks later, the user will have mood swings and feel low. In theory, it shouldn't have a long-lasting effect, but our study showed that even those people who had stopped taking it had higher scores on the depression rating than those who had never taken it.'

Taurah presented a paper yesterday at the British Psychological Society's annual conference in Bournemouth.

At the conference earlier in the week, Dr Fabrizio Schifano, a leading authority on the drug, revealed new data showing how ecstasy was very often being taken in a cocktail with other drugs. Schifano, a consultant psychiatrist at the addiction centre at St George's Hospital Medical School in south London, said: 'What we know from previous studies is that those who take relatively large amounts of tablets have an eight times higher chance of suffering depression than the lower users.'

He revealed at the conference that, out of the 202 ecstasy deaths recorded in England and Wales between 1997 and April 2002, 85 per cent involved mixing ecstasy with other drugs.

He said that it was common for clubbers to start their evening with a mixture of alcohol and ecstasy and that during the second part of the night – usually between 2am and 3am – they would often re-energise themselves with 'uppers' such as cocaine and amphetamines.

Then at the end of the night, as the 'loved-up' feelings begin to fade and be replaced with irritability – usually between 5am and 6am – it was common to take 'downers' such as alcohol and heroin.

'If you take ecstasy, you tend to have a liberal attitude towards drugs and are more likely to have tried a vast array of other drugs, but even when you allow for the impact of the other chemicals, it is clear that ecstasy is linked to depression and other cognitive disturbances.'

He said that most users were completely unaware of the fact that it might also lead to memory loss and difficulties concentrating.

> *For clubbers who are taking large number of tablets regularly, ecstasy actually appears to tip them into clinical depression*

This has been confirmed by brain-imaging techniques showing that ecstasy affects serotonin neurones – nerve impulses fired when the mood-chemical serotonin hits them.

The cells, which run from the brain stem down to the frontal cortex, are 'pruned' by the chemical, removing cells that affect our response to pain and govern mood and cognitive functions.

'We can no longer conclude that ecstasy is going to be safe. This new study confirms the other research showing that even a small amount has an impact,' said Schifano.

'What no one can predict is what it will mean for the future. These clubbers may be 24 or 25, but how will their minds be affected by the time they are 55 or 60?'

■ This article first appeared in *The Observer*, 16 March 2003.

Depression – Q & As

Information from the Association of the British Pharmaceutical Industry

What is depression?

Depression is an illness in which there are thought to be changes in the chemistry of the brain. In particular, small molecules called *neurotransmitters* appear to be present in the wrong amounts or to function incorrectly, thus provoking a variety of distressing symptoms affecting mood, rational thinking and perception. However, depression is more than just a mood disorder. It is a real illness, may have marked physical symptoms (e.g. stomach pains, headaches, rapid heartbeats) and is often a severe, enduring and recurring mental condition which needs active management.

How common is depression today?

Depression is far more common than most people realise and affects an estimated 80 million people worldwide. Studies by the Royal College of Psychiatrists indicate that one person in 20 is suffering from depression at any one time. More than one in five people claim to have experienced depression during their lifetime.

Unipolar depression is common in both sexes, but affects about twice as many women as men in developed countries. By contrast, bipolar disorder affects the two sexes equally. After childbirth, as many as 50 per cent of all women can experience the 'baby blues', and 1 in 10 develops post-natal depression requiring treatment. The seasonal form of depression (SAD) affects about one person in twenty.

Can depression affect anyone?

Depression can affect anyone, but the age of onset is most frequently under 30. Contrary to popular belief, the chance of a first episode of depression does not increase with age – in fact, half the people over 65 who become depressed have experienced some form of depressive illness in earlier life.

In global terms, depression is international and can be recognised

in almost all cultures, though the dominant symptoms vary. This may be due in part to the possible social stigma that would attach to admitting to mental illness.

Can children suffer from depression?

Yes, contrary to general belief, even children under the age of 10 can experience depression. Recent studies show that about one child in every 100 suffers from major depression between the ages of 9 and 11, with boys outnumbering girls. After the onset of puberty, the number trebles and girls become more vulnerable than boys. A tragic consequence of major depression in children is suicide or attempted suicide, especially in the over-15 age group. In the USA, suicide in

children and adolescents increased by four times between 1950 and 1990. Figures as high as 33 per cent for minor depression in children have been reported by some investigators.

What is the relationship between anxiety and depression?

Over the past 40 years, opinions have varied from considering anxiety and depression as two separate illnesses to considering them as a line between 'pure' anxiety and 'pure' depression, with every shade between them. Today, this latter view is the most widely held and the American Psychiatric Association classification of mental illnesses (called DSM-IV) now includes criteria for mixed anxiety/depression. Certainly, many people with severe depression also report strong feelings of anxiety and many people with severe anxiety go on to acquire depressive symptoms and vice versa.

Is depression inherited?

At the present level of our understanding, we can say that people do not inherit depression directly from

Stressful life events

Lifetime experience of stressful life events: by type of event and gender, 2000

Great Britain	Males	Percentages[1] Females
Death of a close friend or other relative	68	73
Death of a close relative[2]	51	55
Being sacked or made redundant	40	19
Serious or life-threatening illness/injury	30	22
Separation due to marital difficulties or breakdown of steady relationship	25	29
Bullying	19	17
Serious money problems	14	8
Violence at work	6	2
Running away from home	5	5
Violence at home	4	10
Being homeless	4	3
Being expelled from school	2	1
Sexual abuse	2	5

1 Percentage of males/females aged 16-74 who reported experiencing each event.
2 Parent, spouse, child or sibling.

Source: Psychiatric Morbidity Survey, Office for National Statistics

their parents. However, it is now clear that some genes can make a person more susceptible to it. For example, studies of identical twins (who possess identical genes) show that if one becomes depressed, there is a 50 per cent chance that the other will as well. The figure is even more startling for bipolar disorder and approaches 75 per cent. For non-identical twins, the risk of both having depression is 25 per cent. The risk of clinical depression is also higher in other relatives than in the general population and as many as 20 per cent of the relatives of a depressed person will also experience some kind of depressive illness. The risk for a child is about 50 per cent if both parents have depression.

Is depression a serious condition?

Clinical depression should always be regarded as a potentially serious condition. Not only is the illness profoundly distressing to the individual, it is damaging to self-esteem, physical well-being, relationships, and careers. Of even greater concern is the link between depression, deliberate self-harm and suicide. In cases of major depression, there is a high risk of suicide or attempted suicide and around 10-15 per cent of people admitted to hospital for depression eventually kill themselves. There are about twenty times as many cases of deliberate self-harm as there are suicides. Many of these will be 'cries for help' and not intended to be successful, but they spotlight the enormity of the anguish that these people are experiencing.

There are about 4,500 suicides every year in the UK, of which 93 per cent are people suffering from some mental illness. This occurs mostly among people who have had depression, which accounts for about 70 per cent, but 15-20 per cent have alcohol-related mental illness, and 3-5 per cent schizophrenia. Many people who attempt suicide have sought help from others, such as their GPs, in the weeks before the attempt, suggesting scope for identifying people at risk and initiating preventive measures. It is for this reason that the Government has made the reduction of suicides one of its key health targets.

It is important that the patients are given and accept advice from their doctor or consultant about their medication

---

Is complete recovery after depression possible?

Yes. It has been estimated that over three-quarters of people with depressive illness will eventually go into remission without treatment. However, in many cases, this may take months or years and clearly a person cannot be left untreated in the hope that they will eventually recover. Unfortunately, there are two particular problems with depression – recurrence and chronic illness.

■ *Recurrence and relapse*: In some people, depression returns at the end of treatment after a period of being completely free of symptoms. This is called a recurrence. The chances of a recurrence are estimated at 50 per cent if the person has no previous history of depression, rising to 70 per cent, 80 per cent and 90 per cent when one, two or three previous depressions have occurred. Others begin to recover while undergoing treatment, but the illness flares up again – called a relapse.

■ *Chronic depression*: Some people (estimated at about 15 per cent) fail to respond to medication and psychotherapy and have what is called resistant depression. In extreme cases, other forms of treatment may then be considered, such as electroconvulsive therapy (ECT) or psychosurgery.

Is the attitude of the patient towards medicines important?

It is important that the patients are given and accept advice from their doctor or consultant about their medication. For example patients need to:

■ appreciate that medicines may be slow to begin to take effect and that they must continue to take them as prescribed

■ watch carefully for signs of recurrence or relapse and seek early advice

■ be assured that medicines for depression do not have the problems of addiction associated with some others used in, for example, anxiety or schizophrenia

■ understand that minor side effects might be experienced, specially at the beginning of treatment.

Can depression be treated without medicines?

Several forms of treatment do not depend on the use of medicines. Two kinds of psychotherapy have proved useful – *cognitive therapy* and *interpersonal therapy*. Overall, the numbers responding are similar to those taking medicines, but the degree of response is greater with medication. The best response seems to be obtained by combining psychotherapy with medication. It has been suggested that both anti-depressant medicines and the various forms of psychotherapy work by breaking the loop in which profound sadness and negative thoughts constantly re-inforce one another.

In cases of resistant depression, especially when there is a high suicide risk, *electroconvulsive therapy* (ECT) or psychosurgery may be considered. ECT has frightening associations, but is beneficial in resistant depression. The patient is given a short-acting anaesthetic, a muscle-relaxing medicine and oxygen, then an electric current is passed through the head from electrodes, which causes a seizure lasting for about 30 seconds. This may be repeated several times over some days. Psychosurgery today is very different from the extreme techniques used in the past. Present practice uses radio frequency waves to produce lesions in parts of the brain involved in the depressive loop, and recovery from the operation is generally very quick.

■ The above information is from the Association of the British Pharmaceutical Industry's web site which can be found at www.abpi.org.uk
© ABPI – *The Association of the British Pharmaceutical Industry*

Symptoms of depression

Information from Depression Alliance

The most common symptoms are set out on this page. If these have been experienced for more than two weeks it is essential to seek help. People may suffer from two or three of these symptoms but are unlikely to experience them all.

- Feelings of helplessness and hopelessness.
- Feeling useless, inadequate, bad.
- Self-hatred, constant questioning of thoughts and actions, an overwhelming need for reassurance.
- Being vulnerable and 'over-sensitive'.
- Feeling guilty.
- A loss of energy and motivation, that makes even the simplest tasks or decisions seem difficult.
- Self-harm.
- Loss or gain in weight.
- Difficulty with getting off to sleep, or (less frequently) an excessive desire to sleep.
- Agitation and restlessness.
- Loss of sex drive.
- Finding it impossible to concentrate for any length of time, forgetfulness. A sense of unreality.
- Physical aches and pains, sometimes with the fear that you are seriously ill.

In severe depression, these feelings may also include:

- Suicidal ideas.
- Failure to eat or drink.
- Delusions and/or hallucinations.

Different types of depression

Some types of depression are very specific.

Severe depression

If the depression is very bad, and the person who is suffering is in need of immediate support, contact the Samaritans on 0845 790 90 90 and your GP as soon as possible. Try to cope by getting support.

Manic or bipolar depression

This type of depression is marked by extreme mood swings, from 'highs' of excessive energy and elation to 'lows' of utter despair and lethargy. Manic depression is often treated with Lithium, which evens out the mood swings.

Post-natal depression

This is not 'the baby blues' which occurs 2-3 days after the birth and goes away. Post-natal depression can occur from about 2 weeks and up to 2 years after the birth.

SAD

Seasonal Affective Disorder is a type of depression which generally coincides with the approach of winter, starting with September and lasting until spring brings longer days and more sunshine.

Information about SAD and light boxes can be obtained from the Seasonal Affective Disorder Association on 01903 814942.

More information

- Depression is much misunderstood by the public, yet it affects many people of all ages. It is estimated that one in five people will suffer from depression at some point in their lives.
- Depression is an illness where the feelings of hopelessness and helplessness, linked to the inability to concentrate, may make it hard for some people to carry out normal daily activities.
- Depression is an illness with a wide range of physical and psychological symptoms, which sometimes make it hard to recognise and understand.
- Personality may play a part in depression. Although anyone can become depressed under particular circumstances, some people seem to be more vulnerable than others. This may be because of things that have happened in childhood, such as abuse, or because of our individual make-up (including body chemistry).
- A lot of effective, intelligent and creative people suffer from depression and yet make an outstanding contribution to life. Often, information about their depression is only revealed after their death, as people misunderstand the illness. Amongst such people are Florence Nightingale and Sir Winston Churchill, who used to call depression his 'black dog'. Depression can affect anyone and does not reduce your value as a human being.

About depression

It is important for people to know that:

- Depression is an illness that can affect anyone at any age.
- It is not connected with and does not develop into insanity.
- Depression can be treated. People may be offered antidepressants and/or talking treatments.
- There is no need to cope alone. Depression Alliance can help.

- The above information is from Depression Alliance's web site which can be found at www.depressionalliance.org

Depression

Information from the Mental Health Foundation

What is depression?

Depression describes a range of moods, from the low spirits that we all experience, to a severe problem that interferes with everyday life. The latter type, sometimes referred to as 'clinical depression', is defined as 'a persistent exaggeration of the everyday feelings that accompany sadness'. If you have severe depression you may experience low mood, loss of interest and pleasure as well as feelings of worthlessness and guilt. You may also experience tearfulness, poor concentration, reduced energy, reduced or increased appetite and weight, sleep problems and anxiety. You may even feel that life is not worth living, and plan or attempt suicide.

Depression can affect anyone, of any culture, age or background. About twice as many women as men seek help for depression, though this may reflect the greater readiness of women to discuss their problems. One thing that may make it hard for doctors to recognise depression is that people with depression often complain of physical problems, commonly headaches, lethargy, stomach upsets or joint pains, rather than low mood, sometimes because these can be significant symptoms, but some-times because they find it difficult to admit to feeling emotionally distressed for reasons they may not even be able to identify.

Depression is usually related to upsetting life events, such as bereavement, relationship difficulties, physical illness, or job or money worries.

Are there different types of depression?

Bi-polar affective disorder (Manic Depression)
Someone with bi-polar affective disorder has both 'high' and 'low'

> *Depression describes a range of moods, from the low spirits that we all experience, to a severe problem that interferes with everyday life*

mood swings, along with changes in thoughts, emotions and physical health.

Post-natal depression (PND)
About 1 in 10 women experience postnatal depression in the first year after having a baby. For further information please see our factsheet on *Post-Natal Depression*.

Seasonal Affective Disorder (SAD)
Some people describe feeling depressed regularly at certain times of the year. Usually this kind of depression starts in the autumn or winter, when daylight is reduced. For further information please see our factsheet on *Seasonal Affective Disorder*.

How can you reduce the risk of depression?

- Keep in touch with your friends. If you are already depressed you find it very difficult to be sociable, and this can make you feel more depressed. So it is important for you to keep in contact with friends and find someone to talk to when you are feeling low.
- Keep active. Being more active is associated with lower levels of

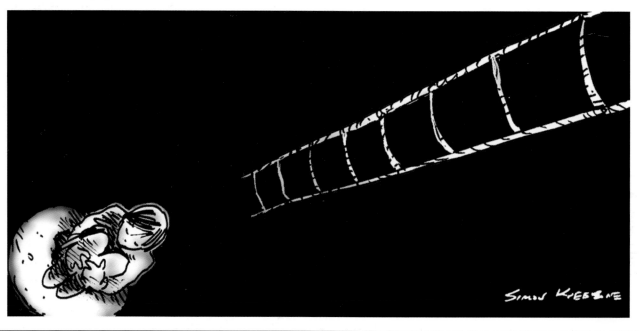

depression. Outdoor activity seems to be particularly important in staving off depression in older men.

- Review your eating habits. Recent research has suggested that people who are depressed may have low levels of certain essential fatty acids, which are found in fish oils. It has therefore been suggested that people with depression should change their eating habits, for example eating more oily fish such as sardines, or should take fish oil supplements.
- Investigate herbal medicine. St John's Wort (Hypericum perforatum) can help many people with mild to moderate depression. Before taking St John's Wort check with your doctor or pharmacist especially if you are taking other kinds of medication, for example for heart disease, epilepsy, asthma or migraine.
- Investigate self-help techniques. Some people have reported benefits from various self-help techniques such as meditation, listening to music, and acupuncture.
- Take control. Some people find it helps if they have some control over what happens. This helps to guard against the kind of 'hopelessness' which is associated with depression. Activities that involve making a 'fresh start' have been shown to help people recover from long-lasting depression. Similarly, learning to set small or manageable goals can give you a sense of achievement and make you feel better.
- Find out more. There are a number of self-help books, guides, and software programs which can help you to learn ways of coping with mild to moderate episodes of depression.

What treatments are there for depression?

Drug treatments

Antidepressant drugs act by increasing the activity of those brain chemicals which affect the way we feel. Antidepressants are thought to help 2 out of 3 people with depression.

Tricyclic antidepressants, such

Depression is usually related to upsetting life events, such as bereavement, relationship difficulties, physical illness, or job or money worries

---

as dothiepin, imipramine, and amitryptyline are often prescribed for moderate to severe depression. These usually take up to two weeks to start working and may have side effects.

Newer antidepressant drugs (SSRIs and SNRIs) target specific chemical 'messengers' in the brain. The most well-known SSRI is fluoxetine (Prozac) but there are several other brands. These newer drugs are popular because they tend to have fewer side effects than older drugs.

Lithium carbonate is sometimes prescribed to people with severe depression. High levels of lithium in the blood are dangerous so anyone taking lithium must have regular blood tests.

If you are prescribed drugs for depression you will probably be advised to take them for at least six months – or longer if you have a previous history of depression. You may experience withdrawal effects if you stop taking antidepressant drugs, particularly if you stop suddenly. These effects can include headache, nausea, dizziness and even hallucinations. Always consult your doctor before stopping taking antidepressants. Do not stop taking

---

medication suddenly as the withdrawal effects may be severe. For further information please see our factsheet on *Medication*.

Talking treatments

Cognitive behavioural therapy (CBT) is a type of 'talking' treatment. It is based on the fact that the way we feel is partly dependent on the way we think about events (cognition). It also stresses the importance of behaving in ways which challenge negative thoughts – for example being active to challenge feelings of hopelessness.

Interpersonal therapy (IPT) focuses on people's relationships and on problems such as difficulties in communication, or coping with bereavement. There is some evidence that IPT can be as effective as medication or CBT but more research is needed.

Counselling is a form of therapy in which counsellors help people think about the problems they are experiencing in their lives and find new ways of coping with difficulties. They give support and help people find their own solutions, rather than offering advice or treatment. For further information please see our factsheet on *Talking Treatments*.

Electroconvulsive therapy (ECT)

ECT is a controversial treatment which is intended only to be used for people with severe depression who have not responded well to medication or other treatments. The person receiving ECT is given an anaesthetic and drugs to relax their muscles. They then receive an electrical 'shock' to the brain, through electrodes placed on the head. Most people are given a series of ECT sessions. Some people say that ECT is very helpful in relieving their depression, although others have reported unpleasant experiences, including memory problems. For further information please see our factsheet on *Electroconvulsive Therapy*.

- The above information is from the Mental Health Foundation's web site which can be found at www.mentalhealth.org.uk

---

The baby blues and postnatal depression

Information from the Association for Postnatal Illness

One in two women who have just given birth experience the baby blues. This article explains why some women feel emotional after a birth and it offers information and advice about the blues and postnatal depression.

The baby blues
After the birth of a baby about half of all mothers suffer a period of mild depression called the blues. This may last for a few hours or, at most, for a few days and then it disappears.

Symptoms of the blues
Many mothers feel very emotional and upset when they have the blues and they cry for no particular reason. They may find that it is impossible to cheer up. Some mothers feel very anxious and tense. Minor problems may cause mothers with the blues to worry a great deal.

Some mothers have pains for which there is no medical cause or they may feel unwell but without any particular symptoms. Most mothers who have the blues feel very tired and lethargic most of the time. Frequently mothers who have the blues have difficulty sleeping.

Possible causes of the blues
The blues may have several causes, some biological and some emotional.

When a baby is born there are very sudden changes in the mother's hormone levels. Some, required during pregnancy, drop rapidly, while others, like those which start the production of milk, rise. These rapid changes may act to trigger the blues.

Many mothers are unprepared for the extreme weariness, which often follows a birth. The weariness is usually due to a combination of factors. In many cases the mother will have been anticipating the birth with some apprehension. This, as well as the physical exertion of the

birth itself, can make mothers feel exhausted. Rest and quiet are most important after a birth. Few mothers get either, as they are busy responding to the needs of the baby, or, when they might be able to rest, they are disturbed by hospital or home routines or by visitors who may stay too long.

Sometimes the baby may have a slight health problem such as jaundice or feeding difficulties in the early days. These problems are very common with new babies, but they cause mothers great anxiety. The problems do settle down as the baby gets older and mothers should try to talk to medical staff and allow themselves to be reassured that the baby will thrive.

What can be done to help a blues sufferer?
Mothers who have the blues should

In most cases the blues last for only a few days and then the feelings fade

be allowed to cry if they want to and allowed to express their fluctuating emotions. If they feel miserable they should not be told to pull themselves together. It can be a great help to the mother if someone listens to her and reassures her that her worries and misery will not last and that she will soon feel better.

A mother who has the blues must have as much rest as possible. It may also help the mother if she is told that the blues are very common and that they will usually pass quickly.

Affected mothers are often over-sensitive about what is said to them by relatives and medical staff. So tact and empathy from the staff can be very beneficial at this time.

Length of the blues
In most cases the blues last for only a few days and then the feelings fade. If the blues do continue and seem to be getting worse then the mother should see her doctor and discuss the problem.

Postnatal depression
Postnatal depression is an unpleasant illness which affects about 10% of

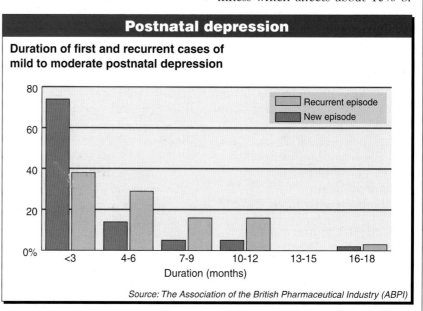

Postnatal depression

Duration of first and recurrent cases of mild to moderate postnatal depression

Source: The Association of the British Pharmaceutical Industry (ABPI)

mothers who have recently given birth. The depression often starts after the mother has left hospital and been discharged by the midwife.

Symptoms of postnatal depression

Postnatal depression has many symptoms. Most mothers who have the illness find that they are less able to cope with the demands of the baby and of the home. Some mothers feel very despondent. They may feel very sad and cry frequently. Some mothers feel anxious and fearful, they worry about their own health and that of the baby. They may suffer from panic attacks and feel tense and irritable all the time. Most depressed mothers feel tired and lack energy, often they feel unable to concentrate and they find even simple tasks are confusing and demand too much energy.

Some mothers experience pains for which there is no cause (other than tension and anxiety), many suffer difficulty in sleeping and poor appetite. Many depressed mothers lose interest in sex.

A depressed mother may suffer from many or all of the symptoms mentioned. Most mothers who have this illness feel guilty that they are not 'coping' as they feel they should be.

What can be done if you have postnatal depression?

If your depression lasts longer than a few days you should discuss your feelings with your doctor. If possible take your partner or a friend or relative with you. Before you see the doctor write a list of all the symptoms that you are suffering from. You should not go on suffering depression in the hope that it will go away. Postnatal depression is a real illness and it can be treated successfully with antidepressant drugs. These

After the birth of a baby about half of all mothers suffer a period of mild depression called the blues

drugs are not addictive. They make the unpleasant symptoms fade until they go completely.

Who else can help?

After you have seen the doctor, you may find it helpful to talk to an understanding and sympathetic member of your family or a friend. If your friend understands that you will recover completely and be your 'old self' again when you are better, then he or she can be a real source of comfort and reassurance to you during the time of your illness.

Your midwife, district nurse and health visitor can also give you advice, reassurance and support.

It is important to remember that all mothers recover from postnatal depression. As the recovery proceeds, the bad days get fewer and less upsetting and the good days become more numerous. Gradually the bad days disappear completely.

Some mothers find it helpful to talk to a mother who has had post-natal depression and recovered. If you write to the Association for Postnatal Illness, we will send you further information about the illness and tell you how to apply for a supporter who has had the illness.

Self-help

Although it may be very difficult to rest when you have a demanding baby and perhaps other children to care for, it does help to rest as much as possible if you are suffering from depression. You will find that you feel worse if you are overtired. Ask a partner or friend to care for the baby

Some mothers find it helpful to talk to a mother who has had postnatal depression and recovered

whilst you have a proper rest, preferably in the middle of the day. Try to lie on your bed even if you do not sleep. A rest in the day often improves sleeping at night for those with sleeping difficulties.

Try to eat a small meal or have a hot sweet drink at regular intervals. Many depressed mothers forget to eat and this can make the depression symptoms feel worse.

If you would like to join a group meeting where all the problems of motherhood are discussed please write to: The National Childbirth Trust, Alexandra House, Oldham Terrace, Acton, London W3 6NR. Telephone 020 8992 8637.

Meet-a-Mum Association, 26 Avenue Road, London SE25 4DX. Telephone 020 8771 5595.

■ If you feel that you are suffering from postnatal depression please read on. If you think that you would like to have one of our volunteers contact you, see our address which can be found on page 41.

■ The above information is from the Association for Postnatal Illness' web site which can be found at www.apni.org

© *Association for Postnatal Illness*

Majority of depressed mothers go untreated

By Sarah Womack, Social Affairs Correspondent

Less than a quarter of women who suffer serious post-natal depression are diagnosed and treated, according to a report.

Most mothers assume they will get better naturally and are unaware that their depression can become a recurring illness.

Doctors are reluctant to prescribe antidepressants due to fears that the medication can be transferred to infants through breast milk.

A report by Datamonitor, the industry analysts, argues the case for widespread medicinal trials to study the differences between drugs already on the market and any problems associated with them.

About eight out of 10 women experience some level of depression a few days after giving birth. This usually amounts to feeling weepy and irritable.

But 10 per cent of this group suffer some form of clinical depression, with about four in 1,000 needing hospital treatment. Up to 50 women a year commit suicide before their child's first birthday.

Those who have suffered post-natal depression include the late Princess of Wales; Jerry Hall, the model and former wife of Sir Mick Jagger; Rachel Hunter, the model and former wife of Rod Stewart, and Judy Finnigan, the television presenter.

By 2020, the World Health Organisation estimates that major depression, of which post-natal depression is a sub-group, will be the second highest cause of death and disability in the world.

Nick Alcock, an analyst at Datamonitor, said: 'The lack of effective diagnosis and treatment presents a danger to the potential mental health of women suffering from post-natal depression.

'As childbirth is one of the major physical, social and psychological stresses of a woman's life, research has focused on determining whether it is a predictor for an increased risk of other psychiatric illnesses.'

He said the risk of developing psychosis in the post-natal period was estimated to increase by 14.5 times, while a study of 35,000 births in America found that patients had a sevenfold increased risk of being admitted to a psychiatric hospital within the three-month period after childbirth.

Yet one of the main problems faced by doctors treating post-natal depression was that little clinical research had been published in this area.

> By 2020, the World Health Organisation estimates that major depression will be the second highest cause of death and disability in the world

Mr Alcock said: 'Antidepressant manufacturers need to outline not just the safety but the efficacy of their drugs. Healthcare systems also need to put into place

guidelines which ensure that screening for post-natal depression is more regular.'

He added: 'Mothers with newborn babies are likely to have high interaction with specialists such as obstetricians, gynaecologists, paediatricians and even health visitors as well as increased use of general health care provision in the immediate period after giving birth. These specialists are in a prime position to diagnose and treat any bouts of post-natal depression.'

Studies also showed the negative effect that post-natal depression had on the development of infants.

For example, depressed mothers were more likely to pin the blame for problem behaviour in their children on the youngsters themselves.

Some scientists believe that women who suffer severe post-natal depression have higher levels of chemicals called thyroperoxidase antibodies in their bloodstream.

This suggested that post-natal depression was not caused entirely by the psychological and emotional turmoil associated with pregnancy and birth.

Heather Welford, of the National Childbirth Trust, said post-natal depression was probably caused by a combination of social and biochemical factors.

She said: 'A simple and non-invasive test, either biochemical or psychological, that could identify women who are more likely to develop post-natal depression would be very useful.'

Women are more vulnerable to post-natal depression if they have a family history of depression, have suffered bereavement in the 12 months before birth or were traumatised by the birth.

Hormone treatments are sometimes given but, according to the Royal College of Psychiatrists, there is no clinical evidence that they work.

Depression

Information from the Health Education Board for Scotland

Very few of us could honestly claim we always feel good about ourselves or are entirely satisfied with our lives. Usually we are content with some aspects of our lives, but not all. We like ourselves in certain respects but not in others. We may be uncertain about what lies ahead of us in the future, but believe that on balance it is likely to be bearable. When we talk about feeling depressed in the everyday sense, we generally mean we have hit a bad patch and are feeling down. In time we emerge more or less intact and continue as before with our lives.

However, the type of depression talked about in this article refers to deep feelings of despair and hopelessness. These can affect both men and women of all ages and from all walks of life. When we experience depression in this way, everything becomes a struggle. We feel bad about ourselves, about everything around us and about the future. Nothing seems worthwhile.

'I no longer felt part of the world I was living in. Everything felt strange and unfamiliar. I didn't know why I bothered going on.'

Each person who is depressed will experience it in their own particular way. It can affect our thoughts and feelings. We may:

- Dislike or hate ourselves.
- Feel we are useless or worthless.
- Feel as if a heavy weight or blanket is bearing down on us.
- Feel numb and empty.

People are affected to different degrees by depression. Some may be able to struggle on with their normal life in the face of a mild form of depression, although everything will require extra effort

- Blame ourselves for all sorts of things which are not necessarily our doing and feel guilty.
- Despair of things ever getting better.

The way we behave and the way our bodies function can also be altered if we are depressed:

- Concentration on even simple tasks can be difficult.
- Making even the smallest decisions can become impossible.
- Our usual sleep patterns may be disrupted so that we wake early and cannot fall asleep again, or we may sleep more than before.
- Appetite for food can also be affected. Some people may find they eat much more than usual and gain weight, whereas others lose all interest in food.
- We may experience physical aches and pains because we are depressed. These can of course be alarming for anyone. However, some people become preoccupied with such bodily symptoms, and this in itself is a sign of depression.
- Our interest in other people and events often wanes when depression takes a hold.
- We may feel more inclined to use tobacco, alcohol or drugs when we are depressed.

'I just wanted to hide away and sleep and sleep. That was the easiest way for me to cope with my feelings.'

'I couldn't make up my mind or decide on anything. My thoughts got so muddled – I couldn't concentrate at all.'

People are affected to different degrees by depression. Some may be able to struggle on with their normal life in the face of a mild form of depression, although everything will require extra effort.

Others of us will be overwhelmed by the feelings of hopelessness and despair. It can even seem as if the only way out is to kill ourselves.

Indeed part of depression is the feeling nothing can help and that we are not worth helping. It can be impossible to imagine things changing in any way. This means that the first and most difficult step towards coping more effectively with depression is to accept that there is a problem and that something can be done about it.

People do usually recover from spells of depression. They may even find they can use the experience constructively as an opportunity to take stock and to make positive changes in their lives as a result.

■ This text is taken from the Health Education Board for Scotland (HEBS) publication *Talking about depression.*

Depression: the facts

Information from Aware

Helping to Defeat Depression

Depression

Depression is a common disorder affecting at least 10% of the population directly at some stage or other in their lives. In addition to the marked impact it may have on many facets of the patient's life and that of the family, mood disorders in their many subtle guises have had a major influence on the artistic, political, religious and financial spheres of most cultures. These brief introductory notes outline the different types of depression and how they are treated. If you would like to know more about the subject you can obtain a recommended reading list from Aware.

What is depression?

The word depression has many different meanings but in a psychiatric context it is used in two specific ways. It is frequently used by patients to describe their feelings of emotional distress and in this sense it is regarded as a symptom. Depression is also a diagnosis which a doctor might make when a patient complains of several symptoms such as feelings of sadness and fatigue, having a disturbed sleep, poor appetite and lack of interest. Though there are many different symptoms present when a depressive disorder is diagnosed the symptom 'depression' is just one of these. Sometimes, however, when a diagnosis of depression is made the patient may not actually feel depressed. In many cases a person who is depressed may not realise the nature of the problem and they may need a doctor to tell them that their excessive fatigue or anxiety is actually depression. Everybody gets feelings of sadness or depression and for most these are short-lived and tolerable. Such feelings, or 'normal depressions', occur most frequently in response to the disappointments of everyday life and to a lesser extent our mood fluctuates with the seasons and in response to hormonal factors. Depression which is particularly

severe or prolonged and is more than the person is able to cope with is considered an 'abnormal depression' or a depressive disorder.

Are there different types of depression?

It is generally accepted by experts that there are different types of depression which can be distinguished by looking at the signs and symptoms of the illness, the person's personality features and his or her life experiences. Various brain wave recordings and hormonal tests also help to identify the particular type of depression the person has.

Types and symptoms

Reactive depression

Reactive depression, the most frequently encountered type of mood change, is an extension of the normal upset feeling following an unhappy event in a person's life. Death of a close relative or friend, family strife or the unexpected loss of employment are some of the events that can evoke an extreme state of un-

happiness. Here the mind's state of sadness is an appropriate response to an unwelcome event. Typically the person with reactive depression will feel low, anxious, often angry and irritable and will tend to be preoccupied with the upsetting event and usually will have difficulty getting off to sleep. This type of depression is usually not particularly severe in that the person will get relief when engaged in some social or leisure interest and will be able to continue with their work which will help to distract them from their upset feelings. This is not to say that it is not a depressing experience for the person concerned. Indeed many patients with this form of depression become preoccupied with suicidal thoughts and may resort to self-destructive acts.

Neurotic depression

Some people are particularly prone to reactive depression; at one end of the vulnerability spectrum is the well-adjusted individual who will only experience a reactive depression when faced with exceptional loss or a profound emotional trauma and at the other extreme is the person with an unstable personality who finds minor misfortunes intolerable. Those who are unable to manage the problems of everyday life in an emotionally efficient manner will experience repeated episodes of reactive depression and these moods are referred to as neurotic depressions. Personality traits which typically pose a psychological handicap in this respect are extremes of perfectionism, timidity, unassertiveness, dependency and narcissism.

Endogenous depression

The next type is endogenous depression witch means depression coming from within. In its pure form the patient is unable to point to any major upsetting event in his or her life that might explain the mood change. As we will see later, although this is primarily a chemical or biological type of depression, traumatic events in a person's life will often have acted as provoking agents bringing the depression to the fore. Unexplained tiredness progressing to fatigue is an early symptom of this form of depression. Other distinguishing features include a sense of hopelessness and despair, self-doubt and low self-esteem, poor concentration and indecision. The patient's night sleep is typically punctuated by frequent wakening and he or she is usually unable to sleep beyond 5.00 or 6.00 a.m. Usually the person feels at his or her worst first thing in the morning. The mental and physical slowness which is so characteristic of this type of depression can make even the simplest task seem impossible, thus affecting every sphere of the patient's life. Endogenous depression, which is sometimes referred to as unipolar depression, can recur in some 50 per cent of instances and the risk of recurrence seems more likely where there is a high rate of depression among the patient's relatives. The more severe forms of this depression carry a major suicidal risk as the patient sees little hope for the future and is preoccupied with negative thoughts about his or her abilities. Such depressions which are left untreated frequently result in suicide. False beliefs or delusions may also be expressed by the patient during the depths of depression. These ideas usually centre on his or her imagined shortcomings and may result in the person making major changes in their life, which they will frequently regret once the depression has lifted. Endogenous depression is quite a common form of depression and is experienced by some three per cent of men and six per cent of women at any one point in time.

Depression of manic-depression

The symptoms of the depression of manic-depression, or bipolar depression, are indistinguishable from those of the endogenous variety except for the unique spells of elation or mania with which it alternates. Elation, the opposite to depression, although usually a pleasurable

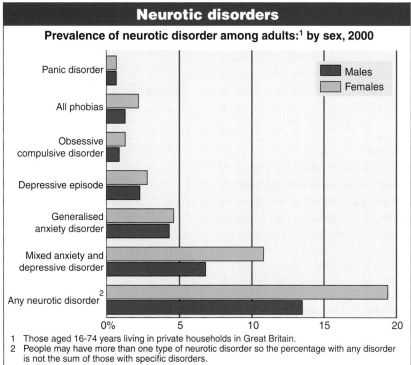

Neurotic disorders

Prevalence of neurotic disorder among adults:[1] by sex, 2000

(Males / Females)

- Panic disorder
- All phobias
- Obsessive compulsive disorder
- Depressive episode
- Generalised anxiety disorder
- Mixed anxiety and depressive disorder
- Any neurotic disorder[2]

(Scale: 0% — 5 — 10 — 15 — 20)

1 Those aged 16-74 years living in private households in Great Britain.
2 People may have more than one type of neurotic disorder so the percentage with any disorder is not the sum of those with specific disorders.

Source: Psychiatric Morbidity Survey, Office for National Statistics

experience, often has just as devastating an effect on the person's life. What makes it particularly serious is that the afflicted individual is often at first quite unaware of their abnormal mood and simply feels uncharacteristically zestful and enthusiastic. In this elated state the patient is overactive, restless, overtalkative, is full of energy and may be involved in a multiplicity of plans and events. Typically they will have difficulty getting off to sleep as they will be unable to 'switch off' their racing thoughts and after only 3-4 hours' sleep will be ready to face the coming day. Initially the person's excessive energy and enthusiasm may be productive, but with time their grandiose plans and impaired judgement can lead to disaster. Heavy drinking, extramarital affairs, overspending, financial blunders are just some of the complications that make mania such a serious disorder. Just as a person who is severely depressed with endogenous depression may experience delusional thoughts, so too may a person who is in an intensely elated state experience false ideas. These are usually of a grandiose quality and concern the person's ability or mission in life. Some 50 per cent of those who have had a one-off episode of manic depression may have a recurrence, but for those who have had a number of episodes

the chances of further recurrence is greater. Some one per cent of the general population will develop this disorder at some stage in their life and typically it occurs between the teenage years and the early forties.

Secondary depression

The final type of depression which can be described is where the mood changes are due to some underlying medical or other psychiatric disorder and this form is referred to as secondary depression. Probably the most familiar one in this category is a depression following a bout of flu. Depression can occur with many other viral infections, anaemias, vitamin deficiencies, thyroid and other hormonal disorders. Certain treatments such as steroids and some blood pressure tablets can also induce mood changes. Schizophrenia is frequently accompanied by depression. Here the mood disturbance often requires to be actively treated in its own right. Alcohol can have a profound influence on mood and for some patients it is a major contributing factor to their depression.

What causes depression?

The different types of depression have different causes and in most instances depression results from a combination of factors coming together at one point in time to produce the mood change. Reactive depression is a response to a major loss in the person's life for which they are usually unprepared. In this situation the person has invested themselves emotionally in somebody or something which is particularly important to them and when they lose this valued relationship the thinking or knowing part of the mind is immediately aware of the loss, while the emotional or feeling part is slower to recognise the change. It is this latter gradual recognition of the loss and the disparity between the knowing and the feeling part of the brain that appears to explain the feeling experienced during a reactive depression. While everybody is vulnerable to this form of depression and will succumb if the stress is great enough, some people, because of previous experiences, are more prone to a reactive depression. For example, somebody who has lost a parent through death but who has been unable to fully grieve this loss may find themselves becoming depressed in response to subsequent but relatively normal losses in their life.

Depression is a common disorder affecting at least 10% of the population directly at some stage or other in their lives

People who experience neurotic depressions have a low vulnerability to stress in that aspects of their personality leave them ill-prepared to deal with the everyday problems of life. Perfectionism leads to disappointments, unassertiveness brings frustration and avoiding situations because of anxiety results in a sense of failure; inevitably repeated exposure to these experiences leads to depression.

Genetic factors are the main casual elements in endogenous depression and manic-depression. Whereas one per cent of the population will develop manic-depression at some stage or other in their life, some 15 per cent of the immediate relatives of a patient with manic-depression will develop a similar illness. Genetic research has shown that the risk increases the closer one is related to the person with the illness; an identical twin has a 70 per cent chance of developing a mood disorder. A variety of different adoption studies have come to the same conclusion and clearly indicate that the major causative factors in these forms of depression are biological ones. However, this is by no means the full explanation. Frequently such bouts of depression will only occur when precipitated by some stressful factor or major change in the person's life.

As well as mentioning the above genetic, stress and personality factors which predispose a person to depression, there are other aspects, such as having a good confiding relationship, feeling in control of one's destiny and being able to tackle day-to-day problems as they arise, which help to protect against mood swings.

■ The above information is from Aware's web site which can be found at www.aware.ie

© Aware

Seasonal Affective Disorder

Information from the SADAssociation

What is SAD?

SAD (Seasonal Affective Disorder) is a type of winter depression that affects an estimated half a million people every winter between September and April, in particular during December, January and February.

It is caused by a biochemical imbalance in the hypothalamus due to the shortening of daylight hours and the lack of sunlight in winter.

For many people SAD is a seriously disabling illness, preventing them from functioning normally without continuous medical treatment.

For others, it is a mild but debilitating condition causing discomfort but not severe suffering. We call this subsyndromal SAD or 'winter blues'.

Symptoms

The symptoms of SAD usually recur regularly each winter, starting between September and November and continuing until March or April, and a diagnosis can be made after three or more consecutive winters of symptoms, which include a number of the following:

Sleep problems
Usually desire to oversleep and difficulty staying awake but, in some cases, disturbed sleep and early morning wakening

Lethargy
Feeling of fatigue and inability to carry out normal routine

Overeating
Craving for carbohydrates and sweet foods, usually resulting in weight gain

Depression
Feelings of misery, guilt and loss of self-

esteem, sometimes hopelessness and despair, sometimes apathy and loss of feelings

Social problems
Irritability and desire to avoid social contact

Anxiety
Tension and inability to tolerate stress

Loss of libido
Decreased interest in sex and physical contact

Mood changes
In some sufferers, extremes of mood and short periods of hypomania (overactivity) in spring and autumn.

Most sufferers show signs of a weakened immune, system during the winter, and are more vulnerable to infections and other illnesses.

SAD symptoms disappear in spring, either suddenly with a short period (e.g., four weeks) of hypomania or hyperactivity, or gradually, depending on the intensity of sunlight in the spring and early summer.

In sub-syndromal SAD, symptoms such as tiredness, lethargy, sleep and eating problems occur, but depression and anxiety are absent or mild.

SAD may begin at any age but the main age of onset is between 18 and 30 years.

It occurs throughout the northern and southern hemispheres but is extremely rare in those living within 30 degrees of the Equator, where daylight hours are long, constant and extremely bright.

Treating Seasonal Affective Disorder (SAD)

Light therapy has been proved effective in up to 85 per cent of diagnosed cases. That is, exposure, for up to four hours per day (average 1-2 hours) to very bright light, at least ten times the intensity of ordinary domestic lighting.

Ordinary light bulbs and fittings are not strong enough. Average domestic or office lighting emits an intensity of 200-500 lux but the minimum dose necessary to treat SAD is 2500 lux. The intensity of a

bright summer day can be 100,000 lux!

Light treatment should be used daily in winter (and dull periods in summer) starting in early autumn when the first symptoms appear. It consists of sitting two to three feet away from a specially designed light box, usually on a table, allowing the light to shine directly through the eyes.

The symptoms of SAD usually recur regularly each winter, starting between September and November and continuing until March or April

---

The user can carry out normal activity such as reading, working, eating and knitting while stationary in front of the box. It is not necessary to stare at the light although it has been proved safe.

Treatment is usually effective within three or four days and the effect continues provided it is used every day. Tinted lenses, or any device that blocks the light to the retina of the eye, should not be worn.

Some light boxes emit higher intensity of light, up to 10,000 lux, which can cut treatment time down to half an hour a day.

Light boxes are not available on the NHS and have to be bought from specialist retailers; they are now free of VAT and start at less than £100.

SADA recommends trying before buying; several companies offer a home trial or hire scheme and SADA has a number of boxes for short-term hire.

Traditional antidepressant drugs such as tricyclics are not usually helpful for SAD as they exacerbate the sleepiness and lethargy that are symptoms of the illness. The non-sedative SSRI drugs such as sertraline (Lustral), paroxetine (Seroxat) and fluoxetine (Prozac) are effective in alleviating the depressive symptoms of SAD and combine well with light therapy.

Other psychotropic drugs, e.g. lithium, benzodiazepines, have not proved widely useful in the treatment of SAD. Daily exposure to as much natural daylight as possible, especially at midday, should help.

Psychotherapy, counselling or any complementary therapy which helps the sufferer to relax, accept their illness and cope with its limitations are extremely useful.

■ Full details of SAD treatment, where to obtain it and how to use it are contained in the SADA *Information Pack.*

■ The above information is from the SADAssociation's web site which can be found at www.sada.org.uk
© SADAssociation

Manic depression

Information from the Manic Depression Fellowship

What is manic depression?

Manic depression is a serious mental health problem involving extreme swings of mood (highs and lows). It is also known as Bi-polar Affective Disorder. Both men and women, of any age from adolescence onwards and from any social or ethnic background, can develop manic depression. It often first occurs when work, study, family or emotional pressures are at their greatest. In women it can also be triggered by childbirth or during the menopause.

The illness is episodic (occurs in phases). It is possible to remain well for long periods. Typically the key to coping with manic depression is an early diagnosis and acceptance of the condition. From this point, self-management, health care, therapy and medication can be taken up as appropriate. Severe and/or untreated episodes of manic depression can be very damaging for all affected.

Mania (high)

Someone experiencing mania may not recognise it is happening. Incoherent, rapid or disjointed thinking or being easily distracted are common features of an episode of mania. Other symptoms may include paranoia and hallucinations affecting vision, hearing or perception. Grandiose delusions or ideas can occur where a sense of identity and self has been distorted by the illness. Sometimes the term psychosis (losing touch with reality) is used to describe these symptoms when they are severe.

Depression (low)

Most people who have a diagnosis of manic depression will experience a severe depression at some time. Usually this will follow an episode of mania where the trauma of the manic episode can sometimes compound the depression. For some people depression will be more likely to occur in the winter months. Symptoms, which are commonly experienced, include a feeling of emptiness or worthlessness (as opposed to sadness), loss of energy and motivation for many (or all) everyday activities, pessimism and negativity about most things (or everything). Thoughts of death and suicide can be common but may be hard to discuss.

Hypomania

Quite often hypomania is explained as a less severe form of mania. Someone who is experiencing hypomania may seem very self-confident and euphoric but may react with sudden anger, impatience or become irritable, sometimes for the slightest reason. S/he may have more ideas than usual, be unusually busy, work too much or be very creative, but not be able to focus on anything for long or switch off and relax. S/he may become more reckless than usual, which might mean errors of judgement at work or in relationships, or be more talkative or challenging with people.

Is there a cause and is there a cure?

Although much progress has been made in understanding bi-polar affective disorder and how it can be managed, research has still not led to either a consensus on the cause or cure. Some research suggests that there is, if not a known genetic link, then certainly an inherited pre-disposition to developing manic depression. It is also known that stressful life events may often precede an episode of mania or depression. As our understanding of the function of the brain increases, more insight can be gained about mood and mental health, and better medications are developed. MDF keeps up with new developments in various research fields and campaigns for more effective research on behalf of those whose lives are affected by manic depression.

■ The above information is from the Manic Depression Fellowship's web site which can be found at www.mdf.org.uk

© Manic Depression Fellowship

Manic depressive illness

Information from the Royal College of Psychiatrists

Introduction

In manic depressive illness, sufferers experience mood swings that are far beyond what most people ever experience in the course of their lives. These mood swings may be low, as in depression, or high, as in periods when we might feel very elated. These high periods are known as 'manic' phases. Many sufferers have both high and low phases, but some will only experience either depression or mania. A more technical term used to describe this illness is 'bipolar affective disorder'. This article will describe both aspects of the disorder, the particular problems they present, ways of coping with them and the range of treatments available. It is a serious condition but, with the right treatment, it is possible to live one's life without too much interference.

How common is manic depression?

It is much less common than simple depressive illness. About one in every hundred adults will suffer from manic depression at some point in their life. It can start at any time during or after the teenage years. Unlike other forms of depression, manic depression affects as many men as women.

What causes manic depression?

Nobody understands this completely, but research has shown that manic depression does seem to run in families, and that it seems to have more to do with genes than with upbringing. It seems that the parts of the brain which control our moods don't work properly – this is why the symptoms of manic depression can be controlled with medication. Episodes of illness can sometimes be brought on by stressful experiences, lack of support, or physical illness. So, it's no use expecting someone with this problem to just 'pull themselves together'.

What does it feel like?

Obviously, it depends on whether the sufferer is experiencing a manic or depressive mood swing.

Depression

Feelings of depression are something we all experience from time to time. They can help us to recognise and deal with problems in our lives. But for someone with manic depression, their depressive feelings will be worse, they will go on for longer and they will make it harder to tackle the daily tasks and problems of living. Someone with this sort of depression will be more likely to have the physical symptoms listed below. Not everyone who becomes depressed will have all these symptoms, but they will usually have several of them.

Mental symptoms
- Feelings of unhappiness that don't go away
- Losing interest in things
- Being unable to enjoy things
- Finding it hard to make even simple decisions
- Feeling utterly tired
- Feeling restless and agitated
- Losing self-confidence
- Feeling useless, inadequate and hopeless
- Feeling more irritable than usual
- Thinking of suicide

Physical symptoms
- Losing appetite and weight
- Difficulty in getting to sleep
- Waking earlier than usual
- Constipation
- Going off sex

If you become depressed you may find that you aren't able to do your job or your normal daily tasks properly. It will become harder and harder to think positively about things and to see a hopeful future for yourself. You may feel like bursting into tears for no reason. You may find it harder and harder to be with other people. In fact, sometimes they may notice that you are not yourself before you have realised there is something wrong.

In mild depression you will usually be able to carry on with some or all of your regular activities. This can be very valuable as it can stop you from getting trapped in a vicious circle of pessimistic thinking that can make you feel worse. But you need to tell someone how you feel, both because that can be helpful in itself, but also so they can help.

■ The above information is from the Royal College of Psychiatrists' web site which can be found at www.rcpsych.ac.uk Alternatively see page 41 for their address details.

The diagnosis of depression

Information from the Association of the British Pharmaceutical Industry

There are no clinical tests yet, such as blood or urine analyses, that correlate with depression and a physical examination will normally reveal nothing unless the depression is secondary to another condition. So great importance is placed on detailed interviews with doctors and/or psychiatrists. These explore such factors as:

- past medical history of the individual
- recent medical history which has led to the consultation with a doctor
- current symptoms
- family history – with the focus on mental illness
- personal history which will explore early development, childhood, educational experience and achievement, career progression, marital status, etc.
- current mental state – focusing on appearance and behaviour, speech, mood, thought control, ability to think logically and correctly, insight
- physical condition
- impairment of social functioning.

The results obtained are compared with diagnostic criteria for mental illnesses that have been

developed by expert panels of psychiatrists and this will allow a diagnosis to be made. Two classifications of mental illness are widely used. The first, developed by the American Psychiatric Association, is called the *Diagnostic and Statistical Manual of Mental Disorders* (Fourth Edition) – usually abbreviated to DSM-IV. The second, ICD10, developed by the World Health Organisation, is called the *International Classification of Diseases* – Part 10 deals with mental illness. Using these guidelines, it is possible to decide which type of depression a person is experiencing and to rule

---

Great importance is placed on detailed interviews with doctors and/or psychiatrists

---

out some other mental conditions which may have over-lapping symptoms.

The depth of depression is gauged from a range of further interviews, tests and questionnaires that the patient may complete themselves or with the help of a psychiatrist or health worker. These will aim to assess various aspects of current mood, degree of risk (e.g. from suicide), mental agility, level of physical alertness, fatigue level, sleep patterns, and so on. One such questionnaire which is widely used is called the Beck Depression Inventory. This consists of 21 questions, each rated for intensity on a scale of 0 to 3, reflecting attitudes often displayed by depressed people. In each, zero represent normality and 3 severe disturbance. Some of the questions used are reproduced in the box opposite.

The Hamilton Rating Scale for Depression (known as HRSD or more often as HAM-D) differs from the Beck Depression Inventory in that it is completed not by the individual concerned, but from observations made of them. It is scored by trained staff who have a knowledge of the person's condition and access to the

clinical interview. This has the advantage that there should be no bias. The results can be plotted graphically, give a snap-shot 'profile' of the individual's condition, and can be used to assess the degree of response to treatment.

A number of other tests may be used which test memory, understanding of spoken language, manual speed and dexterity. Though time-consuming, when taken together, these tests provide a satisfactory degree of confidence in the eventual diagnosis.

Many of these same methods are also applicable to the diagnosis of post-natal depression, seasonal affective disorder and the depressive phase of bipolar disorder. However, the proximity of a depression to a birth, one which shows seasonal fluctuation, or one which alternates with periods of elation and euphoria would point strongly to a diagnosis of depression in any case.

■ The above information is from the Association of the British Pharmaceutical Industry's web site which can be found at www.abpi.org.uk Alternatively, see page 41 for their address details.

© ABPI – The Association of the British Pharmaceutical Industry

Examples of questions used in the Beck Depression Inventory

A. Sadness
1 I do not feel sad
2 I feel blue or sad
3 I am blue or sad all the time and can't snap out of it
4 I am so sad or unhappy that it is quite painful
5 I am so sad or unhappy that I can't stand it

B. Pessimism
1 I am not particularly pessimistic or discouraged about the future
2 I feel discouraged about the future
3 I feel I have nothing to look forward to
4 I feel that I won't ever get over my troubles
5 I feel that the future is hopeless and things cannot improve

C. Sense of Failure
1 I do not feel like a failure
2 I feel I have failed more than the average person
3 I feel that I have accomplished very little that is worthwhile or that means anything
4 As I look back on my life, all I can see is a lot of failures
5 I feel I am a complete failure as a person (parent, husband, wife)

D. Dissatisfaction
1 I am not particularly dissatisfied
2 I feel bored most of the time
3 I don't enjoy things the way I used to
4 I don't get satisfaction out of anything any more
5 I am dissatisfied with everything

G. Self-dislike
1 I don't feel disappointed in myself
2 I am disappointed in myself
3 I don't like myself
4 I am disgusted with myself
5 I hate myself

I. Suicidal Ideas
1 I don't have any thoughts of harming myself
2 I have thoughts of harming myself but I would not carry them out
3 I feel I would be better off dead
4 I feel my family would be better off if I were dead
5 I have definite plans about suicide
6 I would kill myself if I could

L. Social Withdrawal
1 I have not lost interest in other people
2 I am less interested in other people now than I used to be
3 I have lost most of my interest in other people
4 I have lost all my interest in other people and don't care about them at all

P. Insomnia
1 I can sleep as well as usual
2 I wake up more tired in the morning
3 I wake up 1-2 hours earlier than usual and find it hard to get back to sleep
4 I wake up early every day and can't get more than 5 hours' sleep

S. Weight Loss
1 I haven't lost much weight, if any, lately
2 I have lost more than 5 pounds
3 I have lost more than 10 pounds
4 I have lost more than 15 pounds

U. Loss of Libido
1 I have not noticed any recent change in my interest in sex
2 I am less interested in sex than I used to be
3 I am much less interested in sex now
4 I have lost interest in sex completely

■ In total, there are 21 of these items, numbered A to U (only 10 are shown above). After completion, the doctor will add up the total score. From 0-9 is the normal non-depressed range; 10-15 indicates mild depression; 16-19, mild to moderate depression; 20-29, moderate to severe depression; over 30, severe depression.

© ABPI – The Association of the British Pharmaceutical Industry

Diagnosis and treatment of depression

Information from NHS Direct Online

Diagnosis

Depression does not just affect mood, but also energy levels, eating, sleeping and the ability to work and relate to people. It is diagnosed clinically on the basis of the presence of characteristic symptoms. These characteristics are measured using criteria lists, for example, DSM-IV is widely used (*Diagnostic and Statistical Manual of Mental Disorders*) developed by the American Psychiatric Association. When these diagnostic criteria are used, the diagnosis can be made very reliably.

Major depression is:

Over the last 2 weeks, five of the following features should be present, of which one or more should be:

- depressed mood most of the day nearly every day,
- loss of interest or pleasure in almost all activities most of the day nearly every day.

And the remaining (the total to make at least five) from any of the following:

- significant weight loss or gain (more than 5% change in 1 month) or an increase or decrease in appetite nearly every day,
- insomnia or hypersomnia nearly every day,
- psychomotor agitation or retardation nearly every day (observable by others, not merely subjective feelings of restlessness or being slowed down),
- fatigue or loss of energy nearly every day,
- feelings of worthlessness or excessive or inappropriate guilt (which may be delusional) nearly every day (not merely self-reproach about being sick).
- diminished ability to think or concentrate, or indecisiveness, nearly every day (either by subjective account or observation of others),
- recurrent thoughts of death (not just fear of dying),
- recurrent suicidal ideation without a specific plan or a suicide attempt or a specific plan for committing suicide.

And the symptoms cause clinically significant distress or impairment in occupational or other important areas of functioning.

But also:

- It cannot be established that an organic factor initiated and maintained the disturbance.
- The disturbance is not a normal reaction to the death of a loved one (morbid preoccupation with worthlessness, suicidal ideas, marked functional impairment or psychomotor retardation, or prolonged duration suggest bereavement complicated by major depression).
- At no time during the disturbance have there been delusions or hallucinations for as long as two weeks in the absence of prominent mood symptoms (i.e. before the mood symptoms developed or after they have remitted).
- Not super-imposed on schizophrenia, schizophreniform disorder, delusional disorder or psychotic disorder not super-imposed on schizophrenia.

However, depression is often missed, especially when low mood is not the main presenting symptom or when the patient has other illnesses too. To make sure that depression is

not missed, doctors often use screening tests such as the Hospital Anxiety and Depression (HAD) scale. However, not all patients who score positively on a screening test will have a depressive illness and so the doctor still needs to make a proper diagnosis.

Treatment

Treatment for depression usually involves a combination of drug and psychological therapies.

Drug treatments

Antidepressant drugs act by increasing the activity of those brain chemicals which affect the way we feel. Antidepressants are thought to help 2 out of 3 of people with depression.

Tricyclic antidepressants, such as dothiepin, imipramine, and amitryptyline are often prescribed for moderate to severe depression. These usually take up to two weeks to start working and may have side effects.

Newer antidepressant drugs (SSRIs and SNRIs) target specific chemical 'messengers' in the brain. The most well-known SSRI is fluoxetine (Prozac) but there are several other brands. These newer drugs are popular because they tend to have fewer side effects than older drugs.

Lithium carbonate is sometimes prescribed to people with severe depression. High levels of lithium in the blood are dangerous so anyone taking lithium must have regular blood tests.

If you are prescribed drugs for depression you will probably be advised to take them for at least six months – or longer if you have a previous history of depression. You may experience withdrawal effects if you stop taking antidepressant drugs, particularly if you stop suddenly.

About half of the people who have a first episode of depression will have another episode within 10 years

These effects can include headache, nausea, dizziness and even hallucinations. Always consult your doctor before stopping taking antidepressants. Do not stop taking medication suddenly, as the withdrawal effects may be severe.

Talking treatments

Cognitive behavioural therapy (CBT) is a type of 'talking' treatment. It is based on the fact that the way we feel is partly dependent on the way we think about events. It also stresses the importance of behaving in ways which challenge negative thoughts – for example being active to challenge feelings of hopelessness.

Interpersonal therapy (IPT) focuses on people's relationships and on problems such as difficulties in communication, or coping with bereavement. There is some evidence that IPT can be as effective as medication or CBT but more research is needed.

Counselling is a form of therapy in which counsellors help people think about the problems they are experiencing in their lives and find new ways of coping with difficulties. They give support and help people find their own solutions, rather than offering advice or treatment.

Electro convulsive therapy (ECT)

ECT is a controversial treatment which is intended only to be used for people with severe depression who have not responded well to medication or other treatments. The person receiving ECT is given an anaesthetic and drugs to relax their muscles. They then receive an electrical 'shock' to the brain, through electrodes placed on the head. Most people are given a series of ECT sessions. Some people say that ECT is very helpful in relieving their depression, although others have reported unpleasant experiences, including memory problems.

Complications

About half of the people who have a first episode of depression will have another episode within 10 years. There is more of a risk of a further episode of depression than in someone who has never been depressed.

Treatment for depression usually involves a combination of drug and psychological therapies

Mental disorders (particularly depression and substance abuse) are associated with more than 90% of all cases of suicide.

Prevention

To overcome depression and avoid a recurrence individuals should:

- take medication as directed, without skipping any days,
- discuss reducing or stopping medication with their GP,
- gradually try to increase activities they enjoy,
- use the problem solving approach to deal with problems, stresses and worries,
- work on identifying negative thoughts and changing them to positive thoughts,
- assess their symptoms regularly and consult their doctor and/or counsellor if problems arise, and
- try to exercise and get support from a trusted friend or family member.

Side effects

Drug treatments for depression are associated with a number of side effects. Generally, more recently developed drugs (e.g. SSRIs) have fewer and less severe side effects than older drug therapies (e.g. lithium).

Psychological therapies have few, if any side effects. Some other therapies do have some side effects. For example, ECT can result in headaches, memory problems, feeling sick and muscle aches in the short term although it is generally considered very safe.

The Complementary therapy St John's Wort can result in feeling sick, dizziness and a dry mouth.

■ The above information is from NHS Direct and NHS Online's web site which can be found at www.nhsdirect.nhs.uk

© NHS Direct

Do you ever feel depressed?

Information from YoungMinds

We all have to deal with different kinds of feelings and emotions. Sometimes we feel happy and excited. At other times, we'll feel sad and down. There are plenty of things that might make you worry. But people feel and react to different things in different ways. It's normal to feel stressed, anxious or lonely from time to time, or that no one understands us. But for most people, these feelings come and go.

For a small number of people, feeling down or depressed can go on for a long time so they can't get on with their everyday lives.

But if you're feeling down or depressed in any way, then this article is for you.

Why do I feel like this?

'Mum walked out on me and my brother, and dad got a job in another part of the country so we had to move. Mum didn't want to see us any more, because she had a new life. Dad started drinking. It's like I lost everything I knew.'

There are lots of things that can make you feel down or depressed. Here are just some examples:

- If someone close to you is ill, or dies
- worrying about how you look
- feeling guilty or responsible for someone else's behaviour
- worrying about your sexuality
- feeling left out and not being part of a group
- moving or leaving home
- feeling useless and worthless
- arguing with friends or family
- having a parent or carer who is depressed or worried about other things
- changes in your family or becoming part of a new family
- thinking things will get better
- having trouble with your boyfriend or girlfriend, or even just a close friend
- worrying about exams or getting disappointing results
- being bullied at school or elsewhere
- if someone close to you moves away
- feeling you have no one to talk to and that no one understands you
- if you have been abused

How do I know if I'm feeling depressed?

'I couldn't concentrate on my work. I was always daydreaming, and wanted to sleep a lot. I couldn't be bothered to do anything. Sometimes when I felt really low it was scary, and I'd start messing about at school, getting into trouble. Anything not to feel like that . . .'

People show they are unhappy in different ways. It's OK not to feel positive or happy all the time. It's always good to talk to someone about how you feel to understand more and feel more in charge. If you feel like harming yourself it's important to get help.

If it is hard to talk to someone you know, there are a lot of places that offer advice and help

People show they are unhappy in different ways:

- Feeling lazy or bored and tired a lot
- Giving up a hobby or interest
- Arguing with friends or family

- Thinking things will never get better
- Crying a lot
- Having trouble sleeping or having bad dreams
- Lying or making up stories
- Feeling life is not worth living
- Worrying about things
- Being moody or irritable or snappy
- Not wanting to go out
- Feeling no one likes you or people are talking behind your back
- Eating a lot more or a lot less than usual
- Stealing things or getting into trouble . . .

Maybe you recognise some of these in yourself or in a friend.

Ways to help a friend if they're unhappy or feeling depressed

- Listen and try to be sympathetic
- Don't expect them just to snap out of it
- Don't criticise or tease them
- Try and get them to talk about how they feel
- Be patient and allow them time to talk
- Try and help them look for help

Ways to help myself

'After I felt depressed a few times I knew I'd always come out of it, and just tried to do things to distract myself till it passed. That helped a bit. It was horrible thinking it might come back though. In the end I went for counselling, which helped me feel more in control of my life.'

'I didn't think I could talk to anyone I knew. I thought it would just make things worse. I couldn't talk to my friends about it because I didn't think they would take it seriously. I just felt completely alone. I wrote to a problem page and they encouraged me to phone a helpline. Once I did that they helped me have more confidence to get help.'

It's important that anyone who feels depressed finds ways to cope. There are often good reasons why you feel down. So if you're feeling depressed, don't be afraid and don't panic.

And always remember, feeling sad and unhappy will come to an end, even if you sometimes find it hard to imagine. You might find it good to:

- Write a poem or song
- Write things down in a diary
- Listen to some music
- Make a tape of your favourite music
- Do some drawing or painting
- These things may help you understand how you feel

There are lots of other things which might help you feel better, at least for some of the time

The important thing is to do something that you enjoy. Here are just some ideas...

- get outside in the fresh air
- watch something you enjoy on TV
- try a sport like swimming or jogging or dancing – even just go for a walk
- eat regularly and as healthily as you can

Talk to someone

Talking to someone might help you feel more able to cope. Try and talk to someone you like and trust. This might be:

- a friend; a parent or carer; a brother or sister; an aunt or uncle; a grandparent; a friend's parent

Other people you could talk to could be a:

- teacher; school nurse; school counsellor; youth worker; social worker

They may be able to come with you to talk to someone else or may be able to phone someone for advice if you don't want to do it yourself. They may be able to help and reassure you that they sometimes feel the same way. Even if you can't control what is making you feel unhappy – for example, if adults close to you are always arguing, or if someone you know is unwell – it's still important to get help.

If you speak to a teacher they can listen and may give you some advice. If you want, they can speak to someone to try and help sort things out or arrange for you to see a school counsellor. Maybe you have a school counsellor you can see without talking to the teacher.

If you speak to a doctor they should be sympathetic, will listen and should offer you some advice. Sometimes doctors will prescribe tablets, which can be helpful if you are feeling very depressed. They can also refer you to a specialist that is trained to help young people with problems. What you talk to the doctor about will be confidential – that is, they will not tell anyone what you tell them. But if your health or safety is at serious risk then your doctor may want to tell your parent or carer. You may want to speak to your doctor first about this and explain that you want what you say to be confidential.

If you speak to a counsellor or therapist, or someone who is a specialist in young people's difficulties, they will be very sympathetic. They will give you the time to think about what you are going through. They are trained and used to talking to people who have all sorts of worries. They will respect confidentiality and if you agree they may offer to meet you, together with other people who matter to you.

You can also find out about places where young people can go for help through Youth Access.

If you are nervous you can always take a friend with you.

■ *Do you ever feel depressed?*, a pocket-sized, eye-catching colour booklet explains in straightforward language the reasons why, and the ways in which, young people may get depressed. It talks about how normal it is for people to feel up or down at different times, but highlights the difference between feeling like this and more serious longer-term depression which makes daily life very difficult. The booklet deals with the various signs depression and suggests a range of activities which young people may find helpful to combat it. The booklet also lists a number of organisations which they can contact. Price: 55p each.

■ The above information is from YoungMinds' web site which can be found at www.youngminds.org.uk Alternatively see page 41 for their address details.

© *YoungMinds*

For teenagers with depression

Introduction

Been there, done that, bought the t-shirt. Of course, it was over twenty years ago, but I still remember with painful clarity what it was like to be a teenager with depression. The sadness, the feeling of helplessness, the belief that it was part of my personality and the conviction that *something* was wrong. I just didn't know what it was. At that time, in the late '70s, no one really did. The medical community didn't believe children, including teenagers, could suffer from depression. Fortunately, now things are different, to some extent. There still is a lot of mis-understanding about what clinical depression is, so many teens don't get help, either because they don't realise they have depression, or because it's hard for them to get help.

Symptoms of depression
How does it feel?
- You're sad all the time, and/or you feel anxious or numb.
- You feel hopeless about everything.
- You feel guilty.
- You feel worthless.
- You have a lot of physical problems (stomach aches, headaches, chest pain) that don't seem to have any cause.
- You feel irritable (everything and everyone annoys you).
- You have very little energy and you're tired all the time.
- You feel restless and fidgety.
- You have difficulty concentrating on anything.
- You're thinking about suicide or death a lot.

How it may be affecting your life
- Your grades have dropped.
- You're sleeping a lot or having trouble sleeping.
- You've gained or lost weight.

- You don't want to spend time with your friends any more.
- You have no interest in things you used to like doing.
- You cry a lot for no particular reason.

How do I tell my parents?

This is a tough one, and a question I get fairly often. First of all, let's assume that your parents are loving, stable and have your best interests at heart. They may still unknowingly make it difficult for you to get help. They may say, 'What do you have to be depressed about?' or tell you that your feelings will pass and are a normal part of being a teenager. There are two factors at work in this case. One is denial. No parent wants to think something is wrong with their child, especially something like mental illness which has so much stigma attached to it. They may feel guilty or deny what is happening because they feel helpless to take care of you, the way they used to be able to put a band-aid over a scraped knee. The second factor is lack of knowledge on their part. They are not alone in this – over 70% of adults surveyed believed that a depressed person just needed to pull himself/

herself together. In this case, it's not their fault that they don't know enough about depression, and probably just need to be educated. Once you present them with some information, they will probably be eager to get help for you.

I know that you may not have parents like that. Let's assume that your parents are self-involved or have their own problems like addiction or are abusive. In this case you'll have to be strong and get help on your own. It's hard that your parents can't be there for you when you need them, but chances are that you're used to taking care of yourself. If you have depression it's very difficult to do anything positive, but you have to get help. You can't let it ruin your life.

How do I get help?

If your parents are in the first category, probably all you have to do is tell them that you have the signs of clinical depression, and you would like to get a complete physical by your family doctor and get the name of a psychiatrist. If you present them with information about depression and educate them, you can probably overcome their denial and objections fairly easily. They do want what's best for you, and they probably have noticed a change in you.

If your parents are in the second category, you have two choices. One is to find a sympathetic adult who can convince your parents that you need help. This could be a school counsellor, a favourite teacher, your priest or minister, or a friend's parent. You can educate this person about depression if need be and ask them to talk to your parents.

If you can't think of an adult who can help you, go directly to your family doctor and ask for a referral to a psychiatrist. If your family doctor is no help, find a local mental health clinic, suicide prevention centre or crisis hot line. The most important thing is getting treatment; don't let anything stand in your way.

Should I tell my friends?

This is also a tough question. You should realise that this might be something that separates your real, true friends from your not-so-true friends. Some people will be supportive and other people won't, and will probably start avoiding you. But you might want to take negative reactions with a grain of salt. A friend may have a relative who has depression or another mental illness, and that could make it tough for them to be there for you. Or, they may have a sneaking suspicion that they're having problems with their own emotional wellness, and having you confront yours makes them freak out. Don't entirely shut the door on anyone; they may come around in time.

■ The above information is from Wing of Madness' web site which can be found at www.wingofmadness.com

© Wing of Madness Inc.

Getting help

Information from the Royal College of Psychiatrists

Getting help

If you find that your depression is going on for more than a couple of weeks, that it is getting worse or that it is interfering with your normal activities, you should see your family doctor.

Most people suffering from depression get the help they need from their GP. He or she can work out, with you, what sort of help is going to be most useful. In mild depression, counselling may be all that is needed. For moderately severe depression, psychotherapy and/or antidepressants may be needed. For severe depression, antidepressants are usually necessary before psychotherapy can be of help and it usually needs the help of a specialist, a psychiatrist. Only a small number of people with depression ever need admission to hospital. They tend to have depressions that are life-threatening or are just not getting better.

If left untreated, depression can be so bad that life may not seem worth living. You may feel like ending the pain by killing yourself. If you find yourself thinking about this,

THE ROYAL COLLEGE OF PSYCHIATRISTS

LET WISDOM GUIDE

you *must* get help by telling a friend, a professional or the Samaritans. Feeling like this is a phase that many people with depression go through before they get better – it is important to remember that you will get better.

Counselling

This is a way of talking over your problems with someone, a counsellor, who is not involved in your daily life. He or she can help by listening and allowing you to talk frankly in a way that it is sometimes difficult to do with family and friends. A counsellor may be able to help you to get a more helpful perspective on your problems. Putting feelings into words can help you to think about

them more clearly, and to find practical and constructive ways of overcoming problems.

Psychotherapy

There are many different types of psychotherapy. They are all ways of helping people to overcome stress, emotional problems, relationship problems or troublesome habits. What they have in common is that they are all treatments based on talking to another person and sometimes doing things together. Your GP will be able to refer you to a psychiatrist or psychologist for assessment for psychotherapy if this seems to be necessary.

Antidepressants

These are medicines used to treat depression by correcting the chemical imbalance which accompanies depressed mood. The depression caused by manic depression usually requires this sort of treatment. Antidepressants are not simply 'feel-good' pills – they restore the depressed person to a normal mood level but will not improve the mood of someone who is not depressed.

They do have side effects – dry mouth, drowsiness and blurred vision are common with the 'tricyclic' antidepressants. Another kind of antidepressant, the monoamine oxidase inhibitors or 'MAOIs', mean that you have to avoid certain foods such as cheese and red wine. A third form of antidepressants, the 'SSRIs', make some people feel a little sick or agitated when they start taking them. You can find out more about these drugs from the Royal College leaflet on antidepressants. Your doctor will be able to recommend the type of antidepressant that is most appropriate for you.

All antidepressants take between 2 and 6 weeks to work properly. People generally find that their sleep and their appetite improve before their mood lifts. During this period when your mood is still low, support from friends and family is especially important, because it can feel sometimes as if you are never going to get better. You should be seeing a GP or a psychiatrist regularly during this time so that any problems with the tablets can be quickly sorted out.

Even when you are feeling better it is important to carry on taking the tablets as your GP or psychiatrist advises. If you stop them too soon it is more likely that you will become depressed again. If you stop them suddenly, you may have withdrawal symptoms. The general rule is that you should carry on taking antidepressants for 6 months after your depression has lifted. It is advisable to reduce the dose slowly rather than stop the tablets suddenly.

Advice for family and friends
Episodes of mania or depression can be very distressing for family and friends. A manic episode can exhaust all those who are close to the person. Depression can leave family and friends feeling completely powerless to help.

Helping a depressed relative or friend
It is often difficult to know what to say to someone who is very depressed – it may seem that you can't say anything right because they interpret everything in a very pessimistic way. It can be very difficult to know what

they want – this is hardly surprising because often the depressed person does not know themselves what they want. They may be very withdrawn and irritable but at the same time unable to do without your help and support. They may be very worried but unwilling or unable to accept advice. So try to be as patient and understanding as possible.

They may be very withdrawn and irritable but at the same time unable to do without your help and support. They may be very worried but unwilling or unable to accept advice

---

Practical help may be easier to offer and is very important. Make sure that your relative or friend is able to look after themselves properly. If you find that they are seriously neglecting themselves by not eating or drinking, seek medical help immediately.

If they talk of harming or killing themselves, this should be taken seriously and professional help should be obtained.

It is important that you give yourself space and time to recharge your batteries. Make sure that you are able to spend some time on your own or with trusted friends who will give you the support you need at this time. If your relative or friend has to

go into hospital, make sure that you share the visiting with someone else. You will be better able to support your friend or relative if you yourself have had some time to rest.

Helping a manic friend or relative
At the start of a manic mood swing, the person will appear to be happy, energetic and outward-going, the 'life and soul of the party'. They will relish being the centre of attention and will enjoy social occasions such as parties or heated discussions. However, these will tend to increase the sufferer's level of excitement and will tend to make their mood even higher. So, it is a good idea to keep them away from such situations if possible while you try to persuade them to seek help. They will benefit from information about the illness, advice about how to help, and practical support.

If a manic swing has become severe, the person may become hostile, suspicious and verbally or physically explosive. Don't get into arguments but get professional help immediately. You should keep a contact telephone number and the name of a trusted professional handy for any such emergency. There may be times when it is necessary for the manic person to have a short admission to hospital to protect them from getting into trouble.

■ The above information is from the Royal College of Psychiatrists' web site which can be found at www.rcpsych.ac.uk

© 2002 Royal College of Psychiatrists

Doctors fail to spot manic depression

By Jo Revill, Health Editor

Thousands of people suffering from manic depression are having to wait at least a year before they are diagnosed with the condition because many doctors do not recognise the symptoms.

A survey of British psychiatrists to be published tomorrow will show that the illness, also known as bipolar disorder, is still shrouded in mystery, even though it is thought to affect one in every 100 people. Once it has been identified, the condition can be treated with medication and most patients go on to lead relatively stable lives, with little need for hospital services.

But there is growing concern that many are slipping through the net, and spiralling into a deepening depression because they are not treated properly.

One of those who knows how terrible it can be is Sally Earl. At 26, she developed a psychosis linked to the condition immediately after the birth of her daughter. She has had four spells in hospital, and made one suicide attempt, but the mood-stabilising drug Lithium has kept her largely stable, although she says it is a constant battle to stay well, and maintain a steady, quiet lifestyle to avoid the symptoms recurring.

There is growing concern that many sufferers are slipping through the net, and spiralling into a deepening depression because they are not treated properly

'When I was transferred to a mental institution after the birth of my daughter, it was horrible,' said Earl, who is now 44 and has a part-time job as a beauty therapist. 'I was in floods of tears, I felt really desolate and it was as if I hit rock bottom. You cease to differentiate between nightmares and reality.'

She had a further breakdown and developed strange phobias. 'My husband would come home to find that I had thrown lots of things away in the bin. I became convinced that all our net curtains were dirty and had to be washed.'

In a survey of 72 consultant psychiatrists, more than half believed that symptoms experienced in the manic phase are the most damaging to the individual's life. Typically, patients in a manic phase become more active and have heightened mood swings, and exaggerated optimism and self-confidence.

In moderation, these appear to be positive traits, explaining why many sufferers hold down important careers. But when the characteristics become exaggerated, it leads to over-tiredness, excessive irritability and aggressive behaviour.

The disease is often linked to creativity, and has affected several famous personalities, including Spike Milligan. Artists Jackson Pollock and Van Gogh were also said to suffer from the illness, as was Winston Churchill, who famously called it 'black dog'.

Bipolar disorder is a complex mental illness that has an impact not only on sufferers, but also their families and carers. It is estimated to affect more than 1 per cent of the population – nearly 600,000 people.

There does not appear to be one single cause, but several different factors. It tends to run in families and researchers are looking at specific genes which may predispose an individual to the condition, but there are also likely to be environmental factors involved.

Bipolar disorder is estimated to affect more than 1 per cent of the population – nearly 600,000 people

The survey results will reveal that most psychiatrists believe it takes more than 12 months for a diagnosis and one-third of them feel that over half of cases are initially mis-diagnosed, possibly due to a lack of awareness of the symptoms.

If bipolar disorder is mis-diagnosed as depression and anti-depressants are prescribed, they can actually induce manic episodes.

Amanda Harris, chief executive of the Manic Depression Fellowship, said: 'For too long the service needs of people with bipolar disorder have been poorly understood and treatment efforts chronically under-funded.

'The dearth of research into the causes and treatment is remarkable when you consider the cost to society and individuals. Stigma, prejudice and ignorance continue to persist around this illness.'

■ This article first appeared in *The Observer* 12 January 2003.

Treatments for manic depression

What helps?

MDF takes the view that for the majority of people manic depression can be effectively managed with a combination of different approaches: there are a number of mood stabilising medications commonly prescribed for manic depression such as Lithium Carbonate, Lithium Citrate, Carbamazepine and Sodium Valproate. Many people find a combination which suits them through their GP or consultant psychiatrist.

Talking therapies such as cognitive therapy and counselling can often be useful and help recovery. GPs and consultants can make referrals to local practitioners. Learning to self-manage, the principles of which are taught in the MDF Self-Management Training Programme, is for many an invaluable way of learning to manage mood swings and helps to lessen their severity.

Self-help is a tried and tested method, which has enabled many people who experience manic depression to find the help and support they need. Many people also find the support of an MDF self-help group invaluable.

Drug therapy

Drug therapy is an important part of the management of manic depression. Certain drugs suit some people better than others. It is important to be able to discuss your drug therapy with your psychiatrist and GP so that you receive the best treatment available. The more knowledge you have about drugs and other forms of treatment, the better you will be able to put your case.

The drugs used to treat MD can be broadly categorised into:

Mood stabilisers, maintenance therapy, prophylactic drugs

These drugs are used both to treat mania as well as to prevent further episodes of mania and depression. They reduce the extreme changes of mood and activity that are responsible for the disturbances in sleep, appetite, thought processes, judgement and sexual activity that occur in manic depression.

Antidepressant drugs

Antidepressants are used to treat depression, together with a mood stabiliser. They usually take between two and six weeks, or sometimes longer, before they are effective. Close medical supervision is needed, as antidepressants can trigger an episode of mania, SSRIs may be safer in this respect.

Antipsychotic drugs

These drugs are also described as 'major tranquillisers' and 'neuroleptics'. Antipsychotic drugs appear to act chiefly by blocking the action of dopamine, but also affect other chemicals in the brain. They are used to calm and stabilise a patient during an acute manic episode. A mood stabilising drug would also be taken at this time. Rarely, antipsychotic drugs are taken continuously to help stabilise an individual and reduce the incidence of psychotic episodes.

■ The above information is from the Manic Depression Fellowship's web site which can be found at www.mdf.org.uk Alternatively see their address details on page 41.

© Manic Depression Fellowship

Antidepressants

Information from the Royal College of Psychiatrists

What are antidepressants?

Antidepressants are drugs that relieve the symptoms of depression. They were first developed in the 1950s and have been used regularly since then. There are several different types, but this article will concentrate on the older 'tricyclic' anti-depressants and the newer 'SSRIs' (Selective Serotonin Reuptake Inhibitors). These two types account for 95% of antidepressants prescribed. There is a newer group called 'SNRIs' (Serotonin and Nor-adrenaline Reuptake Inhibitors), but these are not yet so widely used.

How do they work?

There are almost thirty different kinds of antidepressants available today. They all work by altering the way in which certain chemicals work in our brains. These chemicals are made by our body and are called neurotransmitters.

Neurotransmitters are the chemicals which transmit signals between the cells in our brains. In depression, some of the neuro-transmitter systems, particularly those of Serotonin and Nor-adrenaline, don't seem to be working properly. We think that anti-depressants work by increasing the activity of these chemicals in our brains.

What are antidepressants used for?

They are used to treat moderate to severe depressive illnesses. They are also used to help the symptoms of severe anxiety, panic attacks and obsessional problems. They may also be used to help people with chronic pain, eating disorders and post-traumatic stress disorder. Don't assume that because you have been prescribed an antidepressant that this means you are suffering from de-pression. If you are not clear about why you have been given them, ask your doctor.

THE ROYAL COLLEGE OF PSYCHIATRISTS

LET WISDOM GUIDE

How well do they work?

Studies have found that after 3 months of antidepressant treatment between 50% and 65% of the people who take them will be much im-proved. This compares with 25-30% of people given an inactive 'dummy' pill, or placebo. It may seem surprising that people given placebo tablets improve, but this happens with all tablets that affect how we feel – the effect is similar with painkillers. Antidepressants do seem to be helpful but, like many other medicines, some of the benefit is due to the placebo effect.

Are the newer ones better than the older ones?

Yes and no. The older tablets (Tricyclics) are just as effective as the newer ones (SSRIs) but, on the whole, the newer ones seem to have fewer side-effects. A major advantage for the newer tablets is that they are not dangerous if someone takes an overdose of them.

Do antidepressants have side-effects?

Your doctor will be able to advise you here. You should always remind him or her of any medical conditions you have or have had in the past.

Tricyclics

These commonly cause a dry mouth, a slight tremor, fast heartbeat, constipation, sleepiness, and weight gain. Particularly in older people, they may cause confusion, slowness in starting and stopping when passing water, faintness through low blood pressure, and falls. If you have heart trouble, it may be best not to take one of this group of antidepressants. Men may experience difficulty in getting or keeping an erection, or delayed ejaculation. Tricyclics are dangerous in overdose.

SSRIs

During the first couple of weeks of taking them, you may feel sick and more anxious. Some of these tablets can produce nasty indigestion, but you can usually stop this by taking them with food. More seriously, they may interfere with your sexual function. There have been reports of episodes of aggression, although these are rare.

The list of side-effects looks worrying – there is even more information about these on the leaflets that come with the medica-tion. However, most people get a small number of mild side-effects (if any). The side-effects usually wear off over a couple of weeks as your body gets used to the medication. It is important to have this whole list, though, so you can recognise side-effects if they happen. You can then talk them over with your doctor. The more serious ones – problems with urinating, difficulty in remembering, falls, confusion – are uncommon in healthy, younger or middle-aged people.

It is common, if you are depressed, to think of harming or

killing yourself. Tell your doctor – suicidal thoughts will pass once the depression starts to lift.

What about driving or operating machinery?

Some antidepressants make you sleepy and slow down your reactions – the older ones are more likely to do this. Some are fine to take when driving. Remember, depression itself will interfere with your concentration and make it more likely that you will have an accident. If in doubt, check with your doctor.

Are antidepressants addictive?

Antidepressant drugs don't cause the addictions that you get with tranquillisers, alcohol or nicotine. You don't need to keep increasing the dose to get the same effect. You won't find yourself craving them if you stop taking them.

However, studies have shown that up to a third of people have withdrawal symptoms for a short time when they stop antidepressants. These include stomach upsets, flu-like symptoms, anxiety, dizziness, vivid dreams at night or sensations in the body that feel like electric shocks.

They seem to be most likely to happen with an SSRI antidepressant called Paroxetine (Seroxat), but can be prevented by slowly reducing the dose of antidepressant rather than stopping it suddenly.

What about pregnancy?

It is always best to take as little as possible in the way of medication during pregnancy, especially during the first 3 months. However, some mothers do have to take anti-depressants during pregnancy. The evidence so far is that their babies don't show any harmful effects from this.

What about breastfeeding?

Women commonly become depressed after giving birth – this is called post-natal depression. It usually gets better with counselling and practical support.

However, if you are one of those mothers unlucky enough to get it badly, it can exhaust you, stop you from breastfeeding, upset your relationship with your baby and even hold back your baby's development. In this case, antidepressants can be helpful.

What about the baby? He or she will get only a small amount of antidepressant from mother's milk. Babies older than a few weeks have very effective kidneys and livers. They are able to break down and get rid of medicines just as adults do, so the risk to the baby is very small. Some antidepressants are better than others in this regard and it is worth discussing this with your doctor or pharmacist. On balance, bearing in mind all the advantages of breast-feeding, it seems best to carry on with it while taking antidepressants.

How should antidepressants be taken?

- Keep in touch with your doctor in the first few weeks. With some of the older Tricyclic drugs it's best to start on a lower dose and work upwards over the next couple of weeks. If you don't go back to the doctor and have the dose increased, you could end up taking too little. You usually don't have to do this with the SSRI tablets. The dose you start with is usually the dose you carry on with.

- Try not to be put off if you get some side-effects. Many of them wear off in a few days. Don't stop the tablets unless the side-effects really are unpleasant. If they are, get an urgent appointment to see your doctor.

- Take them every day – if you don't, they won't work.

- Wait for them to work. They don't work straight away. Most people find that they take 1-2 weeks to start working and maybe up to 6 weeks to give their full effect.

- Persevere – stopping too early is the commonest reason for people not getting better and for the depression to return.

- Try not to drink alcohol. Alcohol on its own can make your depression worse, but it can also make you slow and drowsy if you are taking antidepressants. This can lead to problems with driving – or with anything you need to concentrate on.

- Keep them out of the reach of children.

- Tempted to take an overdose? Tell your doctor as soon as possible and give your tablets to someone else to keep for you.

How long will I have to take them for?

Antidepressants don't necessarily treat the cause of the depression or take it away completely. Without any treatment, most depressions will get better after about 8 months.

If you stop the medication before 8 or 9 months is up, the symptoms of depression are more likely to come back. The current recommendation is that it is best for most people to continue taking antidepressants for six months after they start to feel better. It is worthwhile thinking about what things might have made you vulnerable, or might have helped to trigger off your depression. There may be ways of making this less likely to happen again.

What if the depression comes back?

Some people have severe depressions over and over again. Even when they have got better, they may need to take antidepressants for several years to stop their depression coming back. This is particularly important in older people, who are more likely to have several periods of depression. For some people, other drugs such as Lithium may be recommended. Psychotherapy may be helpful in addition to the tablets.

So what impact would these tablets have on my life?

Depression is unpleasant. It can seriously affect your ability to work and enjoy life. Antidepressants can help you get better quicker. They can be prescribed by your GP and, apart from the side-effects, should have very little impact on your life. People on these tablets, particularly the newer ones, should be able to socialise, carry on at work, and enjoy their normal leisure activities.

If you have been depressed for a long time, others who know you well (for example your partner) may have got used to you being like this. Some people in this situation have reported that, as they got better and developed a more lively outlook, their partners had difficulty in adjusting to the change. This can cause friction in a relationship and is something that people need to be aware of and discuss openly if it happens.

What will happen if I don't take them?

It's difficult to say – so much depends on why they have been prescribed, on how bad your depression is and how long you've had it for. It's generally accepted that most depressions resolve themselves naturally within about 8 months. It is quite possible to get through a mild depressive episode using some of the other treatments mentioned later in this article. If you are in doubt, then you should talk to your doctor.

What other treatments of depression are available?

- It is not enough just to take the pills. It is important to find ways of making yourself feel better, so you are less likely to become depressed again. These can include finding someone you can talk to, taking regular exercise, drinking less alcohol, eating well, using self-help techniques to help you relax and finding ways to solve the problems that have brought the depression on. For some tips on self-help, see our leaflet on depression.
- There are a number of effective talking treatments for depression. Counselling is useful in mild depression. Problem-solving techniques can help where the depression has been caused by difficulties in life. Cognitive therapy was developed to treat de-

pression and helps you to look at the way you think about yourself, the world and other people. For information about these and other forms of psychotherapy, see our factsheets on *Cognitive Therapy* and *Psychotherapy*.

- There is also a herbal remedy for depression called Hypericum. This is made from a herb, St John's Wort, and is available without prescription.
- You may find that you get depressed every winter but cheer up when the days become sunnier. This is called seasonal affective disorder (SAD). If so, you may find a light box helpful – this is a source of bright light which you have on for a certain time each day and which can make up for the lack of light in the winter.

How do antidepressants compare with these other treatments?

Recent studies have suggested that over a period of a year, many of these psychotherapies are as effective as antidepressants. It is

generally accepted that antidepressants work faster. Some studies suggest that it is best to combine antidepressants and psychotherapy. Unfortunately some of these therapies are not readily available within the NHS in some parts of the country.

Hypericum, or St John's Wort, is widely used as an antidepressant in Germany. It seems to be as effective as antidepressants in milder depression, although there is little published evidence for its effectiveness in moderate to severe depressions.

Exercise and self-help books based on cognitive therapy can be effective treatments for depression. If you have any further questions about antidepressants which haven't been covered in this article have a word with your doctor or psychiatrist. It's also good to talk things over with your family or friends.

■ The above information is from the Royal College of Psychiatrists' web site which can be found at www.rcpsych.ac.uk

© 2002 Royal College of Psychiatrists

Antidepressants in common use

Drug name	Trade name	Group
Amitriptyline	Tryptizol	Tricyclic
Clomipramine	Anafranil	Tricyclic
Citalopram	Cipramil	SSRI
Dothepin	Prothiaden	Tricyclic
Doxepin	Sinequan	Tricyclic
Fluoxetine	Prozac	SSRI
Imipramine	Tofranil	Tricyclic
Lofepramine	Gamanil	Tricyclic
Mirtazapine	Zispin	NaSSA
Nortriptyline	Allegron	Tricyclic
Paroxetine	Seroxat	SSRI
Reboxitine	Edronax	SNRI
Sertraline	Lustral	SSRI
Trazodone	Molipaxin	Tricyclic-related
Venlafaxine	Efexor	SNRI

Key
SSRI = Selective Serotonin Reuptake Inhibitor
SNRI = Serotonin and Norarenaline Reuptake Inhibitor
NaSSA=Noradrenergic and Specific Serotonergic Antidepressant

A better pill to swallow

Certain antidepressants can be far more effective than others, reports Oliver James

There is plenty that can be said against taking antidepressants. First, they have side-effects. The modern pills (called SSRIs) have less than the older ones (tricyclics), but, for example, at least half of SSRI-users are liable to a loss of sexual appetite or actual sexual performance problems, beyond what was already due to the depression (depressed people are anyway not very sexed-up).

Secondly, about half of their efficiency is due to what is known as the placebo effect – to wanting to believe it will work. Only a quarter of the improvement is due to the pill, and the remaining quarter the result of 'spontaneous remission' (the patients would have got better regardless of what they took).

And, thirdly, a great deal of the research into their effects is outrageously compromised by funding: nearly all is paid for by the drug companies who produce the pills. They have a huge investment in positive outcomes and can suppress results that have unattractive commercial implications.

> **Definitions of depression and its treatment have been determined by the marketing agendas of drug companies, not by science**

In this connection, it's really worth reading *The Antidepressant Era*, by psychiatrist David Healy. He persuasively (yet readably) argues that definitions of depression and its treatment have been determined by the marketing agendas of drug companies, not by science.

Nonetheless, despite these problems, I have to admit that I have seen many people greatly helped by taking antidepressants. In particular,

I suspect that almost anyone who is really depressed would benefit from a six-month course on an antidepressant just to get them into a state where they can benefit from talking therapy.

When it comes to recommending which pills are best, I am not a doctor myself and have no qualification in pharmacology. But when writing my book *Britain on the Couch (Why We're Unhappier Compared with 1950)*, I interviewed a sample of psychiatrists for their informal views, albeit often supported by the research (for what that's worth).

Almost certainly, you should have an SSRI. Virtually no one should be taking tricyclics today, because they tend to create a mental fug, a weary disconnectedness. However, by contrast, SSRIs usually sharpen the mind.

But which SSRI? The one called Lustral is probably the least worst. I would be very firm with your GP – if they try to give you anything else, unless they can come up with a strong reason, I would absolutely insist. Start on 50mg a day and, after a week, increase it to 100mg.

Quite simply, the alternatives are more likely to give you problems.

For instance, Prozac not only can heighten anxiety to dangerous levels, it is a serious sex-dampener. It is being prescribed a lot at the moment because its cost to the NHS has plummeted, but do not be palmed off with it for that reason.

> **About half of antidepressants' efficiency is due to what is known as the placebo effect – to wanting to believe it will work**

Likewise, Seroxat has had legal action taken against it by 4,000 British users who claim they have become addicted to the drug.

Take my advice and within a few months of getting Lustral down you (no, I do not have shares in the company that makes it), you should be all set for next week's subject: finding the right therapist.

■ This article first appeared in *The Observer*, 2 February 2003.

© Guardian Newspapers Limited 2003

Talking treatments

Counselling that may help

By Kasia Szymanska, Centre for Stress Management, UK

Since the 1950s the profession of counselling has mushroomed. There are now over 400 different types of counselling available. Some of the more common types of counselling include cognitive behaviour therapy (CBT), person-centred counselling, and psychodynamic counselling.

Counsellors see clients in a variety of settings ranging from doctor's surgeries to hospitals and places of work. Clients are often referred to counsellors by their own doctors, psychiatrists or they self-refer, that is they find a counsellor by looking through directories such as the Yellow Pages or directories published by counselling organisations. Sessions are usually once a week, for a fixed period of time and the costs of counselling sessions can vary, clients can expect to pay from £20 to £130 per session (approximately).

Cognitive behaviour therapy (CBT)

One of the most popular, effective and well-researched forms of counselling is CBT. This approach suggests that the way a person feels and how they act is largely determined by their evaluation of situations.

For example, take a fictitious client called Ross who feels uncomfortable when thinking about giving a presentation to his colleagues at work. He has clammy hands, his heart starts to race and his mouth

may be dry. This is not due to the presentation, because otherwise everyone giving a presentation would feel the same way, rather, it is due to his evaluation/unhelpful view of the presentation, e.g. 'I could really mess this one up'. In the case, the cognitive behaviour therapist would help Ross view his meeting in a more realistic light, e.g. 'I've prepared for the presentation and therefore there is no reason why I should mess it up', teach him relaxation strategies and get him to role play the presentation, so he feels calmer and more in control when he gives the presentation.

Assessment is a key component of this therapy; the counsellor often spends the first two sessions gathering information about the client's problem(s) in order to, first, gain an accurate picture of their problem(s). Sessions usually last either 50 minutes or 1 hour and clients are frequently asked to complete exercises between sessions. The counselling is mainly short term, i.e. six sessions plus (although individuals with long-term problems will need more sessions). CBT can be applied to a variety of problems, including anxiety, depression, different types of phobias, sleeping difficulties, chronic fatigue, obsessions, compulsions, substance misuse and Post Traumatic Stress Disorder (PTSD).

Choosing the right type of counselling

As already stated, CBT is one of many approaches to counselling; counsellors who use other approaches work in different ways. For example, psychodynamic counsellors tend to focus on clients' early life experiences and the impact of these experiences on their current problem(s) and would not give clients exercises to do in between sessions.

If you are experiencing problems and think counselling might help, it is a good idea to read up about the types of counselling available and ask your doctor about the type of counselling they recommend before committing yourself to a particular type of counselling. Also, most counsellors will tell you about the approach they use either on the phone or during the first session, then you can decide whether this approach is right for you.

If you are experiencing problems and think counselling might help, it is a good idea to read up about the types of counselling available

What not to expect from counselling

If you do choose to go for counselling, it is important to take into account what not to expect from counselling, such as:

- A miracle cure: counselling can help towards the resolution of problems; however, this can take a number of sessions and motivation on behalf of the client to help themselves.
- Advice: counsellors do not give advice, they help clients to come to their own decisions.
- A friendship or relationship: counsellors are bound by a code of ethics which precludes them from forming friendships or relationships with their clients.

- In this article, the terms counselling and therapy are interchangeable.

- The above information is from STAND's web site which can be found at www.depression.org.uk Alternatively see page 41 for their address details.

© STAND, 2003 depression.org.uk

■ Depressive illness is very common although there are no reliable figures. (p. 1)

■ In Britain, the Royal College of Psychiatrists say that 1 in 20 adults (5 per cent) suffers from depressive illness at any one time, which is broadly similar to the US experience (p. 1)

■ Depressive illness is almost twice as common in women as in men. In Britain, 3-4% of men and 7-8% of women suffer from moderate to severe depressive illness at any one time. (p. 1)

■ Research shows that one in five people in Great Britain experience stress on a daily basis and that the emotional consequences are severe, with a quarter of people who are stressed feeling isolated by it, nearly half feeling depressed or down, and one in eight believing they have nowhere to turn. (p. 2)

■ Depression is a common problem. It affects at least 2 in 100 children under 12 and 5 in every 100 teenagers. (p. 4)

■ Until the 1980s, it was generally thought that children could not become depressed. Now researchers recognise that children, like everyone else, are not immune from this insidious and dangerous disease. (p. 6)

■ A study of 1,600 students in Australia between 1992 and 1998 found that frequent use of cannabis led to depression and anxiety, particularly in girls. (p. 7)

■ Depression is far more common than most people realise and affects an estimated 80 million people world-wide. (p. 9)

■ After childbirth, as many as 50 per cent of all women can experience the 'baby blues', and 1 in 10 develops post-natal depression requiring treatment. (p. 9)

■ It has been estimated that over three-quarters of people with depressive illness will eventually go into remission without treatment. (p.10)

■ *Severe depression*
If the depression is very bad, and the person who is suffering is in need of immediate support, contact the Samaritans on 0845 790 90 90 and your GP as soon as possible. Try to cope by getting support. (p. 11)

■ *Manic or bipolar depression*
This type of depression is marked by extreme mood swings, from 'highs' of excessive energy and elation to 'lows' of utter despair and lethargy. (p. 11)

■ *Post-natal depression*
This is not 'the baby blues' which occurs 2-3 days after the birth and goes away. Post-natal depression can occur from about 2 weeks and up to 2 years after the birth. (p. 11)

■ *SAD*
Seasonal Affective Disorder is a type of depression which generally coincides with the approach of winter, starting with September and lasting until spring brings longer days and more sunshine. (p. 11)

■ It is important for people to know that:
– Depression is an illness that can affect anyone at any age.
– It is not connected with and does not develop into insanity.
– Depression can be treated. People may be offered antidepressants and/or talking treatments.
– There is no need to cope alone. (p. 11)

■ Less than a quarter of women who suffer serious post-natal depression are diagnosed and treated, according to a report. (p. 16)

■ SAD (Seasonal Affective Disorder) is a type of winter depression that affects an estimated half a million people every winter between September and April, in particular during December, January and February. (p. 20)

■ Light therapy has been proved effective in up to 85 per cent of diagnosed cases of Seasonal Affective Disorder. (p. 21)

■ In manic depressive illness, sufferers experience mood swings that are far beyond what most people ever experience in the course of their lives. These mood swings may be low, as in depression, or high, as in periods when we might feel very elated. (p. 23)

■ About one in every hundred adults will suffer from manic depression at some point in their life. (p. 23)

■ Depression does not just affect mood, but also energy levels, eating, sleeping and the ability to work and relate to people. (p. 26)

■ Treatment for depression usually involves a combination of drug and psychological therapies. (p. 27)

■ If you find that your depression is going on for more than a couple of weeks, that it is getting worse or that it is interfering with your normal activities, you should see your family doctor. (p. 31)

■ All antidepressants take between 2 and 6 weeks to work properly. People generally find that their sleep and their appetite improve before their mood lifts. (p. 32)

■ Thousands of people suffering from manic depression are having to wait at least a year before they are diagnosed with the condition because many doctors do not recognise the symptoms. (p. 33)

■ There are almost thirty different kinds of antid-epressants available today. They all work by altering the way in which certain chemicals work in our brains. (p. 35)

■ Studies have found that after 3 months of antidepressant treatment between 50% and 65% of the people who take them will be much improved. (p. 35)

■ Since the 1950s the profession of counselling has mushroomed. There are now over 400 different types of counselling available. (p. 39)

ADDITIONAL RESOURCES

You might like to contact the following organisations for further information. Due to the increasing cost of postage, many organisations cannot respond to enquiries unless they receive a stamped, addressed envelope.

Association for Postnatal Illness
91 Norroy Road
London, SW15 1PH
Tel: 020 7386 0868
Fax: 020 7386 8885
E-mail: info@apni.org
Web site: www.apni.org
The work of the Association is essential as post-natal illness affects between 70,000 and 100,000 women and their babies in the UK every year. It is rightly called 'the silent epidemic'.

The Association of the British Pharmaceutical Industry (ABPI)
12 Whitehall
London, SW1A 2DY
Tel: 020 7930 3477
Fax: 020 7747 1414
Web site: www.abpi.org.uk
The Association of the British Pharmaceutical Industry is the trade association for about a hundred companies in the UK producing prescription medicines.

Depression Alliance
35 Westminster Bridge Road
London, SE1 7JB
Tel: 020 7633 0557
Fax: 020 7633 0559
E-mail: hq@depressionalliance.org
Web site: www.depressionalliance.org
Depression Alliance is a UK charity offering help to people with depression, run by sufferers themselves.

Manic Depression Fellowship Ltd
Castle Works
21 St George's Road
London, SE1 6ES
Tel: 020 7793 2600
Fax: 020 7793 2639
E-mail: mdf@mdf.org.uk
Web site: www.mdf.org.uk
The Manic Depression Fellowship works to enable people affected by manic depression to take control of their lives.

Mental Health Foundation
7th Floor, 83 Victoria Street
London, SW1H 0HW
Tel: 020 7802 0300
Fax: 020 7802 0301
E-mail: mhf@mentalhealth.org.uk
Web site: www.mentalhealth.org.uk
Uses research and practical projects to help people survive, recover from and prevent mental health problems.

Royal College of Psychiatrists
17 Belgrave Square
London, SW1X 8PG
Tel: 020 7235 2351
Fax: 020 7235 1935
E-mail: rcpsych@rcpsych.ac.uk
Web site: www.rcpsych.ac.uk
Produces an excellent series of free leaflets on various aspects of mental health. Supplied free of charge but a stamped, addressed envelope is required.

The Samaritans
The Upper Mill
Kingston Road
Ewell
Surrey,
KT17 2AF
Tel: 020 8394 8300
Fax: 020 8394 8301
E-mail: admin@samaritans.org.uk
Web site: www.samaritans.org.uk
Deals with suicide related issues. Their help line is open 24 hours a day: 08457 90 90 90

SANE
1st Floor, Cityside House
40 Adler Street
London, E1 1EE
Tel: 020 7375 1002
Fax: 020 7375 2162
Saneline 0845 767 8000
E-mail: sanelineadmin@sane.org.uk
Web site: www.sane.org.uk
Funds research into the causes and treatments of schizophrenia. Raises awareness of serious mental illnesses. Produces the magazine, *Sanetalk*. Saneline is the first, national telephone helpline

providing relief to sufferers, support to carers and information to healthcare professionals. Ask for their publications list.

Seasonal Affective Disorder Association (SADA)
PO Box 989
Steyning
Sussex, BN44 3HG
Tel: 01903 814942
Fax: 01903 879939
Web site: www.sada.org.uk
The SAD Association is a voluntary organisation and registered charity which informs the public and health professions about SAD and supports and advises sufferers of the illness.

STAND
Robert Mond Memorial Trust
46 Grosvenor Gardens
London, SW1W 0EB
Tel: 020 7881 9003
Web site: www.depression.org.uk
Through STAND's website, publications, conferences and the development of support groups, it provides accessible information, education, support and better understanding of the most common, yet serious, mental health problems.

YoungMinds
102-108 Clerkenwell Road
London, EC1M 5SA
Tel: 020 7336 8445
Fax: 020 7336 8446
E-mail: enquiries@youngminds.org.uk
Web site: www.youngminds.org.uk
YoungMinds is the national charity committed to improving the mental health of all children and young people. YoungMinds' Parents' Information Service, leaflets, seminars, consultancy and YoungMinds Magazine help young people, parents and professionals to understand when a young person is troubled and where to find help.

INDEX

ACKNOWLEDGEMENTS

The publisher is grateful for permission to reproduce the following material.

While every care has been taken to trace and acknowledge copyright, the publisher tenders its apology for any accidental infringement or where copyright has proved untraceable. The publisher would be pleased to come to a suitable arrangement in any such case with the rightful owner.

Chapter One: Depression

Depression, © SANE 2003, *Stressed Britain*, © The Samaritans, *The emotional effects of stress*, © The Samaritans, *Depression in children and young people*, © Depression Alliance, *Young people and depression*, © Depression Alliance, *Depression on the rise among young*, © Guardian Newspapers Limited 2003, *Childhood depression*, © Undoing Depression, *Young cannabis users at more risk of mental illness*, © Telegraph Group Limited, London 2003, *Ecstasy use triggers deep depression*, © Guardian Newspapers Limited 2003, *Depression – Q & As*, © The Association of the British Pharmaceutical Industry (AMPI), *Stressful life events*, © Crown copyright is reproduced with the permission of Her Majesty's Stationery Office, *Symptoms of depression*, © 2003 Depression Alliance, *Depression*, © Mental Health Foundation, *The baby blues and postnatal depression*, © Association for Postnatal Illness, *Post-natal depression*, © The Association of the British Pharmaceutical Industry (ABPI), *Majority of depressed mothers go untreated*, © Telegraph Group Limited, London 2003, *Depression*, © Health Education Board for Scotland (HEBS), *Depression: the facts*, © Aware, *Neurotic disorders*, © Crown copyright is reproduced with the permission of Her Majesty's Stationery Office, *Seasonal Affective Disorder*, © SADAssociation, *Manic depression*, © Manic Depression Fellowship, *Manic depressive illness*, © Royal College of Psychiatrists, *The diagnosis of depression*, © The Association of the British Pharmaceutical Industry (ABPI), *Examples of questions used in the Beck Depression Inventory*, © The Association of the British Pharmaceutical Industry (ABPI).

Chapter Two: Treating Depression

Diagnosis and treatment of depressions, © NHS Direct, *Do you ever feel depressed?*, © YoungMinds, *For teenagers with depression*, © Wing of Madness Inc., *Getting help*, © Royal College of Psychiatrists, *Doctors fail to spot manic depression*, © Guardian Newspapers Limited 2003, *Treatments for manic depression*, © Manic Depression Fellowship, *Antidepressants*, © Royal College of Psychiatrists, *Antidepressants in common use*, © Royal College of Psychiatrists, *A better pill to swallow*, © Guardian Newspapers Limited 2003, *Talking treatments*, © STAND, 2003.

Photographs and illustrations:

Pages 1, 17, 30: Pumpkin House; pages 7, 12, 21, 23, 26, 29, 34, 38: Simon Kneebone; pages 15, 22, 24, 32: Bev Aisbett.

Craig Donnellan
Cambridge
September, 2003